TOP TO

OFF ROAD

BOTTOM

MARC ELLIS

with Charlie Haddrell

HarperCollinsPublishers

HarperCollins*Publishers*

First published in 2011
by HarperCollins*Publishers (New Zealand) Limited*
PO Box 1, Shortland Street, Auckland 1140

Copyright © Toyota New Zealand Ltd and Marc Ellis 2011

HarperCollins*Publishers*
31 View Road, Glenfield, Auckland 0627, New Zealand
Level 13, 201 Elizabeth Street, Sydney, NSW 2000, Australia
A 53, Sector 57, Noida, UP, India
77–85 Fulham Palace Road, London, W6 8JB, United Kingdom
2 Bloor Street East, 20th floor, Toronto, Ontario M4W 1A8, Canada
10 East 53rd Street, New York, NY 10022, USA

National Library of New Zealand Cataloguing-in-Publication Data
Ellis, Marc, 1971-
Top to bottom / Marc Ellis.
ISBN 978-1-86950-944-6
1. Automobile travel—New Zealand. 2. National characteristics,
New Zealand. 3. New Zealand—Description and travel. I. Title.
919.3044—dc 22

ISBN: 978 1 86950 944 6

Cover and internal design by Kelvin and Genie De Wit
Typesetting by Springfield West
Photography by Juan Mon
Cover photo of Marc Ellis by Luke Farmer

Printed by Printlink, Wellington

This publication is printed on paper pulp sourced from sustainably grown and managed
forests, using Elemental Chlorine Free (ECF) bleaching, and printed with 100 per cent
vegetable-based inks.

CONTENTS

INTRODUCTION

I have always been a massive fan of the Toyota Land Cruiser. As for many Kiwis, the Cruiser has a special place in my heart. The FJ40, produced from the 1960s to the mid-1980s, was always my enduring favourite — always, that was, until the mighty FJ Cruiser came along. The new FJ Cruiser, a retro style reminiscent of the FJ40s, reminds me of one of those chunky Tonka toy trucks we used to play with in the seventies with its meaty, muscular body — and this beauty comes complete with all the mod cons.

As well as a special place in my heart, the FJ40 also has a special place in my memory bank. One of my best mates at varsity, a fulla we called the Doctor of Love, had a lovely mustardy, burnt-orange one, highlighted with a few rust spots — inevitable given it had spent close on twenty years battling the elements by the time the Doctor laid his loving mitts on it — and complete with white mags and a decent set of fat feet. Outside of my Valiant, it was the coolest car in Dunedin and, given it was far and away the most rugged and practical vehicle, was the one we always ventured out with on road trips. It was the ideal vehicle for weekend getaways, surfing safaris, ski trips, fishing, hunting and gathering, nude roadies to Christchurch or beyond, and by a long stretch our favourite pastime: chasing skirt. None of us knew exactly why, but when cruising the city streets in Dunedin, it was like they were paved with gold when we were in the Doctor of Love's Land Cruiser. This thing was a chick magnet.

The mythological and mysterious Doctor of Love aboard his '79 FJ40.

We were always flat out in those days.

I remember one particular roadie to Queenstown where, had we not been in such a robust carriage, atop such a solid chassis, things may have come a little unstuck. The Doctor had volunteered to drive, while the rest of us got into our work, playing silly little games all the way. The tape deck on the Cruiser was blasting the Black Crowes' album *Shake Your Money Maker* — the whole way actually, because somewhere not far out of Dunedin the tape got stuck in there and we couldn't get it out. Anyway, not long out of Roxburgh we decided a little off-roading was in order and before we knew it the Doctor had flown over a cattle stop, through a gate, had engaged the beast into four-wheel-drive and we were doing some paddock work. We then headed up through Coal Creek Flat, along the banks of the Clutha River and up into Knobby Range over some terrain that only a Land Cruiser could negotiate, back down through Fruitlands and up on an old trail to the Old Man Range. It was there that we began to feel we were a tad lost. The track had long since vanished and the landscape, while stunning, had a horribly inhospitable feel to it. As the Cruiser bumped and hopped its way forward with us bouncing around in the cabin like loose nuts in a gearbox, suddenly, and to our great relief, we found ourselves in Butchers Gully and a forestry trail led us to civilization again at Blackmans.

The exhilaration, however, was far from over. As we were heading into Alexandra, a tourist pulled out onto the wrong side of the road and headed straight for us. The Doctor of Love, all lightning-quick reflexes and nerves of steel, pulled his left hand down and we swerved into the gutter and came flying out the other side. Flying literally, because all four wheels left the ground and, sooner than we could all take a breath, we had crashed through a fence and bounced to a halt in a paddock. A disaster had been sidestepped. Miraculously, the Land Cruiser was still fully functional and suffered only minor panel damage. After all the reporting formalities we were back on the road and that evening enjoying the Queenstown nightlife. The Land Cruiser loyally transported us up and down the mountain for the weekend — in fact the Doctor of Love spent all weekend taxiing young female backpackers up and down the Remarkables — and back to Dunedin. I believe the Doctor retired his FJ40 out to Great Barrier Island where, legend has it, it is believed to still be towing fishing boats in and out of the water.

It was memories like that one that meant I had a special affinity with Toyota's Land Cruiser. I am also an admirer of Toyota New Zealand's spirited advertising campaigns and the kaizen attitude and philosophy of continuous improvement. So when the blokes at Toyota approached me with the challenge of driving the length of New Zealand, top to bottom, off the road in a smoking-hot new FJ Cruiser to celebrate sixty years of the Toyota Land Cruiser I leapt at the chance and grabbed it with both hands.

The greater Toyota marketing team had developed a way to launch a car that was totally innovative and new in New Zealand, and possibly the world. A way that would build on Toyota's core brand values. A way that would set the benchmark for some time to come. A way that would interactively engage the public through social media to not only follow the campaign but to guide and direct it and fully evaluate the vehicle's performance. It was a campaign that carried risk. A campaign that was alive and unfolding unpredictably. A campaign that would touch people the length and breadth of the country. A campaign that is a true test of character. It was humbling and daunting at the same time. But it was brazen, it was a serious challenge and it was to be a road trip like no other. So I was all over it like a cut and polish.

Little did I know the journey would bring me into contact with some of New Zealand's most colourful characters, iconic Kiwis — the very people Toyota so brilliantly showcased and depicted in their *Everyday People* marketing campaign. These people are living proof that the Kiwi spirit is alive and kicking hard. They welcomed me and the crew to their world. These people *Believe*.

BEFORE THE TRIP: PREAMBLES, PREPARATION AND PROMOTION

So, would you believe it, the good fullas at Toyota New Zealand asked me to test drive the new Toyota Land Cruiser FJ. And they wanted me to take her on a bloody long test drive at that! The length of the country no less. From the very top right down to the very bottom. But I had to do it off-road. Some idea those mad hatters in the Toyota marketing team and their agencies had had, apparently.

So one early summer's day, just before Christmas, we headed to Makoura Lodge, in the foothills of the Ruahine Range in Manawatu, to see just how well the new FJ Cruiser could go — and, just quietly, so I could get a few four-wheel-driving tips. It was there I was introduced to what would be my home away from home for nigh on three weeks. I came face to face with a fully pimped-out FJ Cruiser in 'sun-fusion' yellow, with the traditional white roof, and with no accessory spared whatsoever. This baby, the spiritual successor to the FJ40 of the sixties, seventies and eighties, has a four-litre, double-overhead-camshaft V6 engine with electronic fuel injection, providing 380 newton metres of torque and delivering nearly 200 kilowatts of grunt — in old-school talk that's the power of 260 horses, for crying out, Father Peter! Out of respect for the generations of faithful FJs before it, the new FJ Cruiser's classic retro styling features include wrap-around rear-quarter windows, round headlights buried in the front grille and flared wheel arches — all throwbacks to the legendary FJ40.

My first encounter with what was to be my home for nearly three weeks.

It came complete with the latest Hema Navigation GPS system — fat lot of use that is when you're driving down riverbeds, up sand dunes, through swamps, forests and bush and over farmland, but fun to play with no less. It had a nine-tonne winch, in the unlikely case we needed to pull ourselves out of the shtook, and this snorkel-like thing up the side of the cab, which I took to mean we could take it into the water up to about head height like a submarine. And the interior was as tough and robust as the exterior, with water-resistant upholstery, body-coloured panels and essential tools such as a built-in compass so you don't forget where your north is, inclinometer so you don't get too 'tilty', and an outside temperature gauge so you know whether to wind the window down or not. Plus some pretty damn cool stuff too, like all the Generation Y applications and — I love this — eight stereo speakers including some in the ceiling panels so you can really turn the cabin into a mobile disco if you happen to be feeling that way inclined.

But what I wanted to know was: is this piece of machinery all for show or is she capable of taking me from Cape Reinga to Bluff across some of the harshest, hairiest unsealed terrain in the country?

Well, for a start the FJ Cruiser's got nine inches of ground clearance — pretty bloody good, but I had a funny feeling we were going to need every nine of those inches. Above that it's stacked with protector plates to keep the cooling and steering systems cosy, and to make the body unyielding, uncompromising and unalterable (flash words for rigid) the FJ Cruiser uses specially placed reinforcements and high-tensile strength sheet steel. Another bonus is that it comes with assisted active traction control — a quick-thinking, computer-controlled braking system to control each wheel independently and distribute power to where it's needed most to help with handling when you get into some tricky and sticky situations — and it has a rear differential lock for when things get really gnarly. And 'the Beast', as we

had endearingly termed it, had more lights on the roof than the newly rebuilt Eden Park! As the jokers at Toyota said, 'Think of what New Zealand's great outdoors can chuck your way and rest assured the FJ Cruiser has what it takes to help get you up, over, through, or around virtually any obstacle.' All very well, but I needed to test that claim for myself …

I put her through her paces all right. Up hill and down dale. Took her to what I thought was the limit. And she responded perfectly. Never missed a beat. At times we were on only three wheels, and others even just two!

Forwards, backwards, sideways, but always steady as she goes. Careering down 45-degree shingle slopes didn't faze her one little iota. I even tried to submerge her by plunging into a river and driving upstream. Dangling my mitts out the window, the water was spraying up into them like a high pressure shower.

We popped out the other side of the river no problems whatsoever. I even took her up a muddy track the locals call 'the mudslide' — and displaying brute force the Beast was totally unstoppable.

By the end of the session I was totally blown away by the FJ Cruiser's performance and handling. This thing can go anywhere, over any terrain, wet and muddy, dry and dusty, up, down or sideways. The excitement of the Top to Bottom Challenge had almost started to get the better of me!

If that wasn't stirring enough, my next stop was at the Toyota Signature Class plant in Thames, where a group of experts painstakingly restore pre-loved Toyotas to their former glory or simply give them a touch-up and a tune-up and sort out any defects so they can pass a rigorous inspection to meet Toyota's exacting standards. The visit was exciting because I was to witness and help to restore a beautiful FJ40 Land Cruiser that first rolled off the production line in Christchurch way back in the seventies with a massive workload ahead of it. FJ40s like this one ended up in some of the most remote corners of the country.

They had tough and demanding lives, so there was probably not a heck of a lot of time for much TLC. But for that particular survivor from Rotorua, things were about to change. It received a bolt-by-bolt, ground-up restoration with absolutely no detail spared. The entire chassis and cab were stripped back for a bare metal respray and then rust-proofed to boot. Forty bloke hours all up just for that! And about a half of one of those hours was me. There was no way they were going to let me loose on a set of ratchets so I was relegated to the sealed paint booth — but only to put on a coat of primer, not the top coat.

The motor got a bloody good going over too, and one of the jokers at Signature Class reckons the old girl had one million miles left in her! And every panel, piece of trim and electrical fitting was meticulously reworked by the Thames Toyota Signature Class team in a total refurbishment. At smoko, they used to just stand around and admire the progress and beauty of this old beast.

By the end, the net result was the most stunning, canary-yellow FJ40 since they rolled out of the Toyota factories around the world forty odd years ago. An absolute minter!

This heartbreaker was the coolest old-school ride in the country and some lucky bugger, who was going to help me and the team out, was going to win it!

The end result.

Introducing Captain Trunky.

It was there I also met Captain Trunky — what was to become our trusty support vehicle for the others in the Top to Bottom crew. The Captain was affectionately so named because of the enormous trunk-like safari snorkel mounted up the side of the cabin, moving the engine's air-intake point from a relatively low and vulnerable location under the bonnet to a much higher and safer position for when one gets a little overexcited at water hazards. Captain Trunky was a Toyota Land Cruiser LC70, the boxy-looking model that has been a loyal workhorse for Kiwi farmers, miners and forestry workers for three decades. It comes with a 4.5-litre V8 turbo diesel with heaps of low-down torque.

The ideal wingman for my FJ Cruiser.

And another great thing about old Trunky was that the cab was separated from the tray by a mesh grille, meaning that if anyone overstepped the mark, got out of line, committed an indiscretion or was just having a grumpy day they could ride in the dog-box at the back where those in the back seat could jab them with a cattle-prod until they settled down or had served their time.

I paid a visit to North Shore Toyota to meet Mark Jago, Lewis Rowe, Bruce Taylor and Prem Chand, the team there, where the Top to Bottom FJ Cruiser generated no end of interest. They were generous with their advice on tactics I should employ to get myself the length of the country in one piece. There was one last job to do prior to departure on the Top to Bottom Challenge, though — and that was to equip the FJ Cruiser and Captain Trunky so that every eventuality was planned for. We had a feeling that the good old Kiwi sense of humour might lead us down a few dead ends and we may end up in a spot of bother on the odd occasion. So to counter this we asked New Zealanders to submit ideas as to what we should carry with us and what might come in handy on a challenging journey such as that on which we were about to embark.

The team at North Shore Toyota.

We got some superb suggestions. I read every single one. If the truth be known the best ones came courtesy of the girls. Keri reckoned some kitty litter and chocolate would come in handy — the kitty litter to absorb moisture and provide some grit if the wheels got stuck, and some chocolate for the mid-afternoon sugar rush. Crissy suggested I pack a good old thick pair of pantyhose — great for a quick fix for a broken fan-belt, for use as a fishing net, or to sneakily slip into as a pair of thermals. To that I'd add that pantyhose would be useful for gagging annoying crew members, or as a mask for any breaking and entering stunts. Polly, Trish and others recommended baby wipes — good for cleaning the car and oneself. Not silly advice at all.

There were plenty of calls for dunny paper — most suggesting two-ply, the only reasonable option. As well as recommending goggles and a snorkel, Kawa-tapurangi reckoned I should take plenty of Lemon and Paeroa, Moro bars and pack a thermos of Milo every day. Bruce wished me well, told me how lucky I was to be seeing the remotest parts of the most beautiful country in the world and advised me to take my own camera to snap some personal shots. Mark wasn't thinking along the same lines, though, as he thought we should take a toilet seat that attaches horizontally to the tow-bar. Muriwai suggested a pig dog. And he wasn't the only one. George also believed a dog was a good idea, but his rationale was so there was something to blame for odd smells, urgent pit-stops and bad driving. Neil thought we ought to pack some dental floss. No other single product has so many uses from self-administered stitches to an impromptu, makeshift fishing line he reckoned. Neil also gave

Jerry cans — essential.

Autokraft come to the party with supplies.

some prudent advice — a pillow to jam between the driver's seat and driver's door — my right hip was grateful for that I can tell you. Ritchie thought extra windscreen wiper blades would come in handy as the dirt and foliage would wear them down. Sensible suggestion indeed, that one.

RD1, the rural and dairying supply retail centre, was the obvious first stop for anyone contemplating driving the length of the country off-road. We picked up a couple of jerry cans, one for petroleum and the other for diesel — should we get caught short and not make it to a gas station in time. Spades, picks, cans of CRC 5-56 (aka the liquid screwdriver) and first-aid kits for each vehicle went into the trolley. I also grabbed the largest chainsaw the store had (together with a big tub of chain lube), as well as a tomahawk for clearing the way — or even a spot of pig hunting. Safety is paramount on a journey like this, so I picked up the loudest possible high-visibility vest I could find for me and all the crew — in fluorescent, glow-in-the-dark orange and yellow. I also stocked up on a few obvious necessities like birdseed and a machete. It goes without saying that every vehicle needs those items handy at all times.

Next stop was Kathmandu for a few creature comforts like a sleeping bag, tent and a powerful headlamp (thanks to Jared for that little gem of advice). The crew wouldn't let me chuck in a hammock, blow-up bed or barbecue, which I thought was a little harsh of them. I was only thinking of them, naturally. All I felt was really missing was a chiropractor to bring along to straighten me out at the end of every day's dicey driving.

The day before we left I scanned the Top to Bottom website again — and a really big thanks to all those who wished the whole Top to Bottom team well on this epic journey. It was motivating to read the support we had, suggestions for routes and offers of help and company along the way. It also took away some of the mild anxiety I was feeling given that my wife, Agustina, was due to give birth to our second child — two short weeks after the challenge was due to finish in Invergiggle. And we all know number two can come early …

THE DOCTOR OF LOVE

The Doctor of Love is a legend all right. And his mustard Land Cruiser was too. He called it the Rover Disposer. But that was only one of its nicknames. It was our mobile home while we were up to all sorts of no good in the Scarfie days.

A slight setback occurred on one particular surf trip with the Doctor of Love in the early nineties. As we motored north through Waipu on the promise of an epic late summer storm swell something unusual occurred. We spied a massive avian predator up ahead and soon realized it was a hulking great hawk enjoying some fresh road kill in the middle of the road. The Doctor presumed it would take flight and get out of the way of his Land Cruiser, which was hurtling along directly towards it at about 100 kilometres an hour. We watched from the cab — and it felt almost like an unstoppable object heading straight for an unmovable one. The hawk appeared unflappable (literally!) with such a huge and imposing vehicle bearing down on it. When we were about ten yards away, the

hawk took flight (one can only assume the roadkill was exceptionally tasty) and, bugger my days, came hurtling straight through the windscreen, which shattered into pieces, and joined the Doctor and me in the front seat! Pandemonium ensued until the huge hawk, which seemed intent on having us for pudding, negotiated its way out of the windscreen it had come flying into, not before slicing the Doctor's hand with its lethal talons, and with a bit of a wobble, and no doubt a splitting headache, the bloody thing flew off!

We had to continue the drive on to Sandy Bay with a little more air conditioning than we had bargained for, which wasn't all bad actually as the bird had, among all the excitement, managed to deposit some pretty large droppings throughout the front of the cab before leaving us.

These days the Doctor of Love brings in all sorts of high-net-worth hobnobs from around the world to visit this fine land of ours. He's upgraded his Land Cruiser, though.

DAY ZERO
20 February 2011

The Top to Bottom Challenge was actually due to start on 21 February at Cape Reinga but, to be precise, the journey started the day prior as we left Auckland and pointed the decked-out FJ Cruiser northwards.

The vehicles were packed, the journey prepped and a rough course set for our nineteen-day trip from Cape Reinga to Bluff, where a celebratory dozen oysters and a blisteringly cold Speight's were on order for 8 March. For now, though, we were heading in the wrong direction — and this day spent getting to the start line was going to be a harbinger and a 'taster' of what we had in store over the course of the next few weeks.

Saying goodbye to the family.

We started playing with the CB, and when we tuned into a taxi company's frequency we played havoc with their order system.

Some rare road time before we got into it proper.

As we made our way north, our first stop (and the first chance for the public to get up close, cosy and personal with the FJ) was Whangaroa Harbour where we were set to meet up with legendary Kiwi fisherman Matt Watson. Within a couple of minutes of being there the local publican tracked down Matt on the marine radio. He was out fishing around the point, had a boatload of freshly caught fish and was at least thirty minutes off.

The marlin being brought ashore.

Well! What a thirty minutes! First up, the marine-radio loudspeaker blurted into life and informed those within earshot that a marlin was on the way into the harbour and needed to be weighed. The wharf filled with eager anglers keen to catch a glimpse of the prize, as local kids participated in a bombing competition off the jetty, voted on by the decibel count of the whooping and the shrieks of laughter from their mates.

The fish was hauled up onto land and photos of the crew and angler were snapped for posterity. And what was the chance, but the angler was called Steve Ellis?! No relation, or not that we could quickly identify, but with a bit of tricky little camera work, I positioned my own carcass in front of his first name and so officially had my first marlin — with the photo to prove it.

190 kilograms of marlin.

At the same time the pub had emptied out and the people from the wharf made their way to have their first glimpse of the Top to Bottom FJ Cruiser. It would be fair to say that the car was getting as much attention as, if not more than, the marlin. That was until we draped the marlin over the bulky bonnet of the FJ to even things up.

Matt had radioed in and, as good fishermen do, he had just got on to a school of kingis so his ETA had become a moving target. I'd have loved to have hung around — the Whangaroa Harbour has real charm. One of the Maori immigration canoes, *Mahuhu-ki-te-rangi*, explored the harbour, as legend has it, and early European whaling ships docked here too. And this afternoon had a great buzz going on. My namesake Steve Ellis and his mates, Adam Livingstone and Isaac Kane, were no doubt going to settle in for a celebratory session. But we needed to keep moving.

With no spare time we had to hit the road for Houhora where we would give a few key media a look over the FJ during dinner at the Houhora Big Game and Sports Fishing Club, perfectly situated on the hill above the wharf. The minute we rolled the FJ into the dinner a local launch, named *Chargé d'Affaires*, pulled up to the wharf and was met by a lovely looking 1973 FJ40, owned by the local fish smoker called Frank Goodhue. The media who had gathered there were convinced we had set this up to showcase the new FJ Cruiser beside its predecessor, but that was actually not the case at all. It was pure coincidence. Frank was there to collect another marlin; this time a whopping great 190-kilogram one! That's nearly twice as heavy as Tony Woodcock, for goodness' sake!

My very own big-game trophy.

FRANK GOODHUE

What about Frank Goodhue? Frank's the joker we met at the Houhora Big Game and Sports Fishing Club who'd come to pick up a massive marlin to smoke. He's been smoking marlin, snapper and other bounty from the deep blue for over ten years. He's a chip off the old block. His old man plied the same trade in Paihia many years back. **Way back, Frank used to charter deep-sea fishing boats, but he then turned to his calling — smoking the good stuff.** Frank goes everywhere with his best mate, China the dog. China is so named because when she was young she never stopped digging holes. These days she likes cruising in the Cruiser and helping Frank smoke his fish.

He is the proud owner of a '73 FJ40 Toyota Land Cruiser. He bought it from a panelbeater up north who had done plenty of work on it, including giving it a mostly fibreglass body, but who needed the cash after his marriage broke up, and wanted to get rid of it, quick smart. Frank had seen it a few years before he bought it and had said to this panelbeater that if ever he was thinking of selling it to give Frank a buzz ... and Frank's had it ever since.

Frank Goodhue's FJ40 and the FJ Cruiser. A 38-year age gap, but best of mates.

Frank had owned his FJ40 for about twenty-five years and simply couldn't see a reason to sell it, 'unless the new one comes out with a tray', he reckoned. He had run the local smoking business for years and was only too happy to take another angler's pride and joy away on the back of his Land Cruiser.

The skipper of *Chargé d'Affaires* was a fulla by the name of Robert Aukett. Twenty-seven years as a painter by trade in Okura, Robert is also a key member of the Bay of Islands Swordfish Club. He'd had a pretty good week by the time we saw him pull up to the wharf to be fair — this was his third blue marlin and he'd also grabbed three striped marlin in seven days. With all the energy and excitement in the air, a cracker evening ensued.

But before we could get too over-excited we hit the hay, knowing we needed to be up at sparrow's fart for the start of the Top to Bottom Challenge. We were being sent on our way live on TVNZ's *Breakfast* show so needed to be looking our best and in top shape.

Frank Goodhue's lovely FJ40 taking another catch to be smoked.

OPPOSITE PAGE: A young girl climbed up to get a better view of proceedings.

DAY ONE
21 February 2011

Day One started at 5 a.m. as we drove up to the Cape Reinga Lighthouse. Our goal for the first day was to navigate to Ninety Mile Beach through a marshy headland and to then head down the entire 'ninety miles', beating the tide through to Dargaville. Sounds easy, right?

The sunrise over the Cape was absolutely stunning. There wasn't a cloud in the sky and a light, low mist was hovering over the headland. I'd be lying if I said there weren't any butterflies fluttering in the tummy. I distinctly remember, at one stage, looking straight into the headlights of my Cruiser and, if the truth be known, I even murmured under my breath, 'It's you and me, pal. I sure as hell hope you're up for it!'

Behind us was the iconic lighthouse, built in 1941 and manned until 1987 when the last lighthouse keeper was swapped for some automation — controlled by a link to Wellington, would you believe? Hopefully, sooner rather than later, it'll be granted World Heritage status, because it sure as eggs deserves it. For those who have been to Cape Reinga, they'll appreciate that it's a pretty spiritual place up there where the Tasman Sea meets the Pacific Ocean. Little wonder, as according to Maori mythology, the spirits of the dead begin their journey to the afterlife with a leap off the headland there. (My bet is that the dismount of choice would be either a honeypot or a gorilla bomb.)

Kicking off the epic journey before dawn breaks.

Neeraj Lala and Steve 'Tank' Prangnell from Toyota were there to wish us well.

Excitement, nerves and anticipation got the adrenaline flowing.

CAPE REINGA TO DARGAVILLE

Giving some of the locals a lift.

How many kids can you squeeze into a Land Cruiser?

But for us it was the start of a different journey: to the bottom of the South Island. And only off-road. Word had spread and we were welcomed at New Zealand's northernmost point by dozens of kids and a number of elders from the local kapa haka group, who sent us on our way with a rousing farewell, but not before squeezing fourteen young kids into and onto my Toyota — surely a Guinness world record. Also there were members of the Kaitaia Four Wheel Drive Club, a raggedy bunch of good old buggers, who had got up at 4 a.m. to drive up to the Cape from Kaitaia (now that's commitment to the cause!) and who offered me no end of advice on where and where not to venture. I was starting to get a little anxious about the folkloric Te Paki stream bed. Every time it was mentioned people would smile nervously and tell some fanciful story without looking you straight in the eye. Rumour had it that it was a quagmire of quicksand capable of swallowing whole tour buses in a matter of minutes. What then would happen to my Toyota Land Cruiser? Only time would tell …

A spine-tingling haka to send us on our way.

It was an early morning for these Northland kids.

Harihona 'Uncle' Rata thinks it's funny that someone would want to take his photo.

We got no further than the car park when we were met by a fair group of Land Cruiser owners keen to escort us through the hazardous waterways and onto Ninety Mile Beach. One fulla, from the same proud family as the legendary late Matiu Rata, named Harihona Rata, but affectionately called Uncle by most, was the first to greet us in true Northland style and also loaded us up with a ten-litre tub of bush honey. He ran his own hives and harvested (with his own hands) a special blend of manuka honey which, among other things, had healing properties — bound to come in handy on a trip such as this. And apparently the further north the honey comes from, the better the medicinal properties. Not only that but he had hooked us up for lunch at Hukatere Lodge, about thirty miles down Ninety Mile Beach. What a bloke! And a beaut storyteller to boot. They certainly have plenty of time for you up north.

Our support crew of locals, who had come to ensure we negotiated the tributaries to the beach and beat the tide to Dargaville, came in all manner of machines. Many were Toyotas and most were sporting unique well-worn looks.

WILLIE DARGAVILLE

Willie Dargaville was so keen to join his mates from the Kaitaia Four Wheel Drive Club on their trek to the Cape to see the launch of the FJ Cruiser Top to Bottom Challenge that he'd arranged to buy an old FJ40 from a bloke near Kaitaia. But when he went around to pick it up and pay for it, this fulla had just given it to his nephew who was in need of some wheels so had asked his uncle for a favour and been gifted the Land Cruiser in return. However, it was only a minor setback for Willie, or the Maori Mad Max, as we affectionately nicknamed him. **He had had an old FJ40 up on blocks for about six years so decided it was time to get it ready — and time was short.** Good thing Willie's favourite pastime is tinkering with old cars and doing up old wrecks.

He worked on it while others were sleeping and relied on the odd mate coming over to give him a hand. Mates like Brett Christensen, who works with Willie at the Juken New Zealand Ltd Triboard mill. Juken is a Japanese-owned forestry company and Triboard is a three-layered wooden panel with a wood-strand core sandwiched between MDF outer skins. Willie works twelve-hour shifts, four days on and four days off.

When we caught up with him and his wife Debbie Knight, it was his FJ40's maiden voyage and, according to Willie, it was touch and go as to whether or not it'd make it from Kaitaia to Cape Reinga and back. Good job he thrashed it along Ninety Mile Beach then …

A local legend who shapes surfboards.

37

HARIHONA RATA

What a beautiful man Hari (or Uncle as he is known to most) is. Not that he thinks so, though. When we first tried to catch him on film he said, **'What the hell are you taking a photo of an ugly bugger like me for? There are some gorgeous German birds over there — go and photograph them. They're a damn sight better looking than I am!'**

Uncle is a beekeeper and runs some beehives in Te Hapua, near the shores of the Parengarenga Harbour, producing some of the most sought-after manuka honey in the world. He reckons he's forgotten how many times he's been stung — doesn't really bother him except when he gets a clobbering for getting a bit cocky and going in inappropriately dressed. His brother was also into beehives but of a different sort. The late Matiu Rata was a Minister of Maori Affairs and an MP from 1963 through to 1980.

Uncle had just harvested some high-grade honey when we left from the Cape and said to us, 'Well, you may as well have some of the bloody stuff.' He then said he'd have a chat to Gabrielle Pfaender who runs Hukatere Lodge, and that we should pop in there for a graze as it's right on Ninety Mile Beach. So that we did! Uncle was fairly insistent that we all head back to his part of the world sooner rather than later so he can show us around the local beaches and bushes that hold so much allure. No doubt that we will do.

Taking the Beast for a surf on Ninety Mile Beach.

Willie Dargaville, the Maori Mad Max.

Willie Dargaville's FJ40.

The Boogie Man — Patrick Reha.

Willie Dargaville was running a Land Cruiser with a full roll cage and a Chevy 350-cubic-inch V8 which went like the absolute clappers when warm, but like the crappers when cold or hot. His FJ40 had been off the road and up on blocks for six years until a week before the Top to Bottom Challenge and he had hauled some long hours after work to get to the start line. Legend. He and his wife Debbie were classic folk and spent the best part of the day trying to overtake us — at pace. We almost let them once or twice.

The drive down Ninety Mile Beach was almost unreal. We were escorted, at breakneck speed, I might add, by all manner of Toyota four-wheel-drives. The only other Land Cruiser that looked as good or bad as that of the Maori Mad Max (depending on your view) was owned by Brett Christensen who rode with his cobber Boogie, also known as Patrick Reha. Theirs was more an endurance machine capable of going anywhere but at a more sedate pace. Brett reckoned he'd owned his 'luxurious girl', a rust-coloured FJ40, for over ten years.

LIVING LEGENDS

ROBIN BRACEY

Robin Bracey is a lovely bloke. Born and bred in the Far North, he and his wife have owned Kaihu Motors on State Highway 12, a garage, workshop, service station and store, for twenty-three years. **He is the owner of a remarkably well looked after FJ40, which he has rebuilt from scratch with a five-speed Toyota gearbox powered by a 350-cubic-inch Chevrolet V8.** He's had a few Land Cruisers in his time has old Robin. He's always been involved with four-wheel-drive vehicles, ever since his old man had Willys Jeeps in the fifties. He uses his FJ40 Land Cruiser for recovery work — mostly towing broken down cars back to the garage.

We came across Robin at Maunganui Bluff. Originally, we thought he was our guide to take us back to Dargaville off-road. He sure looked the part. But Charlie caught up with him later and he said, 'Nah, they ran into me by pure fluke. I was just minding my own business when I saw this dolled up new FJ Land Cruiser roaring towards me chucking up a cloud of dust. Then I saw a clown get out of the driver's seat and he came over to me, asked me who I was and we had a bit of a natter.'

BRETT CHRISTENSEN

Brett Christensen is a true-blue Cruiser head. **His 1974 FJ40 Land Cruiser runs an unmodified 4.2 Blueflame six-cylinder motor, housed in a fibreglass body. He drives it every day, any day, all the time — and it never stops.** He takes it on the very odd occasion he needs to go hob-nobbing in town, when on the farm, at the beach and with the Kaitaia Four Wheel Drive Club doing trails. Like his mate Willie, the Maori Mad Max, he works at the Juken Triboard mill and has a pretty cool job. He drives a 13,000-kilogram front-end loader for a living. Basically, anything that gets in his way is history. The same principle applies to his FJ40. His favourite pastime is smashing down scrub, tea tree, bracken, gorse and to continue driving … Top bloke.

It wasn't going to stay this clean for long.

Next stop was Dave 'n' Rose's Sandsurfing at the giant sand dunes at Te Paki. Dave Spicer is from the Far North tribe Ngati Kuri, descendants of Pohurihanga, who sailed the waka *Kurahaupo* to the northern tip of the North Island. Dave and his wife Rose live in Te Hapua, a community on the shores of the Parengarenga Harbour, and have been hosting the sandsurfing at Te Paki for about eight years. They hire out boogie boards to tourists from all over New Zealand, including school groups, and all over the world from Europe to South America. Dave reckons the sandsurfing is transformational in that even the most timid and meek individual feels chest-beatingly pumped after the dune plummet and stream plunge. I certainly believe him on that!

What a blast! Dave was first off. His parting words were, 'Watch my instruction!' I think I knew what he meant. Off like a shot, he got up a hell of a head of steam as his boogie board glided down the massive dunes like a hovercraft at real pace until it slid across the river below the forty-five-degree gradient. I could only follow his lead … after 'watching his instruction'.

Gabrielle, Uncle and others put on some terrific tucker.

Gabrielle Pfaender was all smiles as she
put on a memorable feast.

Just as the tummy started rumbling, our convoy headed into the sand dunes and
made its way via a challenging little sand road to Hukatere Lodge. Our host, Gabrielle
Pfaender, had travelled to New Zealand on a holiday years ago and had fallen in
love with the untouched north and the local characters. Her stunning lodge was the
logical place to stop. It's a grand old colonial-looking building which is completely
self-sufficient in power and water, and Gabrielle's gorgeous horses graze in the
grounds. Gabrielle had headed up to see us off at the Cape, and being a close friend
of Uncle's had invited us all to pop into the lodge for a graze ourselves.

A 'sweeper' catches the Beast as we headed for Ahipara.

We bunkered down and enjoyed an amazing lunch, including fresh farm eggs and the best wild pork I have ever tasted, washed down with a few cups of tea and some fresh fruit, during which we were regaled with stories about the Far North and the inhabitants, which ensured enough of a thread was sewn to guarantee that we would venture back on a return jaunt soon thereafter. The people up north are the key asset of the region — on par with the incredible landscape. They had so much time for us, and were wearing smiles which sometimes seem too few and far between in the big smoke. I reckon that smile comes from knowing that you are in the right place with the right people and you have a feeling that life will unfold just as it ought to.

I could have easily snuck into one of the comfortable-looking rooms at Hukatere Lodge for a sneaky little siesta (some of the Kaitaia Four Wheel Drive Club were having a little shut-eye on the deck) but alas no — no peace for the wicked. After lunch we farewelled our first group of chaperons, and set about racing the tide to Ahipara. You really need to get the timing right here as the tide, particularly a high spring tide as we struck, comes all the way up to the sand dunes, leaving no place to scarper. There are too many vehicles that have fallen victim to the unrelenting surf of Ninety Mile Beach. At one stage the spring tide maxed out and forced us right up into the sand dunes. Even when it was receding we encountered a few 'sweepers'. Although only an inch or two high, sweepers can spin a fifty-seater tourist bus, so we executed plenty of caution and were a bit wary when they came creeping up close. Toyota New Zealand would not be happy in the slightest if the car lasted only fifty miles of this legendary celebration of the Toyota Land Cruiser's sixtieth birthday.

OPPOSITE PAGE: There was no time to dilly-dally.

As Ahipara approached, my apprehension at falling prey to the surf was replaced by a genuine concern about my first challenge to gain valuable 'tarseal credits' that would allow me to link the off-road journey together. Given the need to cross the roads on the very odd occasion, the decision was made that, as driver, I had to endure some form of challenge to earn credits to pass over sealed roads. The web community following the journey on www.toptobottom.co.nz were asked to offer suggestions, which they very kindly did in their thousands! It was pretty darn clear that the only appropriate challenge in Ahipara was to hook up with Garry Sommerville, the legendary founder of Kaitaia Fire — the magical little pepper sauce that put an end to the dominance of Tabasco in New Zealand. As fortune would have it, he had just harvested his habanero chillies and thought it only appropriate that in order to pass, I should consume three of these hand-selected bangers …

Garry Sommerville gives me a bit of background on Kaitaia Fire and tells me no one has ever eaten three raw chillies.

What started off so well hits me hard in the lips, throat, nose, gums, pharynx and oesophagus — not in that particular order.

Now, may I start by saying that I have experienced my fair share of pain, but forcing three habaneros down your gullet is one way of testing your threshold. It's the burn that keeps on giving — and then gives a bit more. The first minute was excruciating and every minute on from five to thirty was a blur of agony and light-headedness, interrupted only by the support crew's laughter and then futile attempts at assistance by way of every conceivable form of liquid, from flavoured milk to frozen Frujus — all of which only spread the burn to my lips, nostrils and beyond. I could have sworn that even my teeth seemed to sting! I completely lost control of my gob and the dribble and drool and tears flowed freely. In the middle of this, my interest as to whether the FJ Cruiser could handle the eighteen-day journey was replaced by a genuine concern as to whether I would.

I think I've swallowed a uranium spill.

The water only aggravates it and besides I have lost all control of my mouth.

LIVING LEGENDS

GARRY SOMMERVILLE

Good old Garry Sommerville, eh. He's the wise guy with the Toyota Hilux from the Far North who had the smart idea that to earn some tarseal credits, I needed to masticate and ingurgitate three of the fieriest *Capsicum chinense* grown on this planet.

Now I love hot food. I've never had a lamb vindaloo I couldn't finish — and people have tried hard to break this record. But boy oh boy ... During the initial couple of chomps on Garry's chillies the sensation was similar to that of a fresh red pepper from the supermarket. But it was after about twenty seconds that I could taste nothing but pain, and shortly thereafter a couple of the crew, worried about my well-being, tried to perform the Heimlich manoeuvre on me. By then my ears were ringing, I'd lost sight in one eye and everything from my neck up was numb. I'd deserved the chance to take to the tar — that's for bloody sure.

Garry's actually a top bloke. So passionate was he about his chillies that he tried to convince me it was a great way to load up on vitamin C. Personally, I'd opt for an orange juice or a kiwifruit over that uranium spill sensation any day. However, what he does with his chillies I really love. You see, Garry is the owner and founder of Kaitaia Fire, which makes New Zealand's favourite accompaniment for barbecues and Bloody Marys — a sizzling hot and delightfully delectable pepper sauce. It's a great substitute for salt, pepper and tomato sauce in any recipe or dish. Garry reckons he has it on everything except pudding and breakfast cereals. He was brought up in Fiji so it's no coincidence he loves things hot, with the Indian influence up there. But when he came back to New Zealand **he couldn't understand why we didn't have a decent fiery pepper sauce of our own, so he went about setting that straight.**

It took some balls, and he had his share of doubters in the early days, but Garry now has a network of organic chilli growers whose crops thrive in the rich peat soils surrounding Lake Ohia. The lake, by the way, was drained by gum-diggers in the late nineteenth century and prior to that was home to a kauri forest before the area was drowned some 30,000 years ago. These crops are used to make the mighty Kaitaia Fire sauce, and Garry has also developed Waha Wera (Maori for 'burning mouth'), a kiwifruit, manuka honey and habanero pepper sauce which is truly mouth-watering — and winner of the World's Best Hot Fruit Sauce at the Fiery Foods Challenge in Albuquerque, New Mexico, back in 1996. To top it all off he's written a book, *The New Zealand Chili Handbook*. What a bloke!

I love the way he signs off on the Kaitaia Fire website:

'We'd be lying if we said that we had dedicated our lives to bringing you, the consumer, great taste sensations. In truth we lead full and varied lives, always striving to maximize the pleasure we get from life, while keeping in mind the number 1 principle in karmic theory — What goes around, comes around.'

Tarseal credits bloody well earned (in fact I personally felt the chilli stunt was enough for me to drive all the way to Wellington on the roads), we continued on, but not until we had helped a local lad retrieve his horse which had bolted on him and run a few kilometres down the main road to a paddock where it could see its girlfriend over a few fences. Who knew horses were romantics?

Marc and the local lad find the horse.

Reunited.

But no sooner had we got on the road when a joker by the name of Kamahl Frost pulled up alongside us with his partner and said, 'I thought you fullas weren't allowed on the road. I'll show you a good short cut.' And with that he was manoeuvring his Toyota Hilux down a fairly tricky little entry point back onto the beach, sideways at times, and encouraging us to follow. We needed no second invitation and tailgated him as he navigated his way through a few rocky outcrops, bouncing around all over the show. We followed Kamahl as far down the beach as possible and it was only when we stopped to farewell him that we realized he had a baby strapped in a car-seat in the back. Lo and behold, the baby was still asleep — quite miraculous given the rough and rugged ride it had just been on!

Kamahl had his baby well strapped in the back of the Hilux, but that didn't stop him showing us the way over torrid terrain.

LIVING LEGENDS

KAMAHL FROST

Now this guy is as tough as teak, is Kamahl Frost. He drives a Hilux 'coz it's as reliable as'. His favourite hobby is thrashing it up and down the beach and it takes as much as he can give it — and some more. His missus had seen the official start of the Top to Bottom Challenge on TVNZ's *Breakfast* show that morning and had decided they should catch up with us for a butcher's hook and see what all the fuss was about. And, as we later discovered, they did so complete with a baby strapped in the back! Kamahl had wondered, **'How does that Marc Ellis fulla land a job trying to wreck a brand new car?'** So it'd be fair to say he was pretty pissed off when he finally did catch up to us to see we were on the road, and seemed to choose not to understand when I told him I had just eaten some true, raw Kaitaia Fire in order to be able to do so. He had better ideas and promptly directed us back off the road. His parting advice was, **'Drive it like you stole it, bro!'**

All I could do was knock the scab off this beer and pass it on.

The sand gave way to dirt back-roads and en route to Maunganui Bluff we crossed the Hokianga Harbour on the Rawene Ferry. There's something soothing about a ferry ride and this was a moment to reflect and regather our thoughts. We were about four hours behind our scheduled meeting time to catch up with Ian Russell, who had been farming the coast for a decade or so and knew every inch of the 110-kilometre beach run down to Dargaville that would bring Day One to an end.

We found Ian at Dave and Gay Duder's. They have a cracker bach overlooking the beach and we had a cuppa and yarn about the trip and the alterations they had just completed to their holiday home. (Dave generously gave beers to those in the crew fortunate to not be driving, but as we had an intrepid journey ahead, I lucked out.) It is a magical spot and on a good day, such as we had, was scintillatingly spectacular. Dave told us that it could cut up pretty rough, as can most west coast beaches, and that when you take the boat out you need to have a good understanding of both weather and tides if you want an uneventful return to shore.

Personally, the crew and I were just happy to be only 100-odd kilometres from a good night's kip after a long first day. Ian led us down the beach toward Dargaville, past a few surfcasters. It's fortunate there aren't any traffic cops on the beach as we were doing well just to keep up with him! He was motoring like a bat out of hell, and as I said he knew every inch, which was lucky as there are numerous soft spots which can be like quicksand if you are going slow and pretty iffy if hit at speed. I found out on the way that Ian was a relative on my mother's side — little wonder he was such a good sort.

Shortly thereafter Day One was over, some seventeen hours and 300 kilometres later. You do the maths — not very fast, eh?

LIVING LEGENDS

GAY AND DAVE DUDER

Gay and Dave Duder were the good folk who asked us into their beaut bach at Maunganui Bluff on the rugged west coast of Northland. Gay and Dave are kumara farmers in Aratapu, about ten minutes out of Dargaville and some forty minutes from their bach — which they access by getting onto the beach at Glinks Gully, not far from the farm, and then driving up the beach, occasionally stopping to go for a fish or to collect a few mussels. **Both were raised in the area and grew to love the Bluff,** so when there were a few rumours about a derelict house overlooking the beach that was

coming onto the market, they were in like Flynn and have never looked back. They don't get to the bach quite as much as they'd like, though, as kumara farming is a hell of a busy occupation. When we came through they were in the middle of the harvest. In the off-season Gay told me they run sheep on the farm, fattening them up, which is great because it keeps the farm tidy and the sheep naturally fertilize the land for the following kumara season. And it can't be all that bad a job. One of Dave and Gay's sons has followed them into it and has his very own kumara farm near Dargaville.

BEN HAIG AND MARARA MURRAY-HAIG

Marara Murray-Haig was born and bred in the Far North. Ben Haig was born and bred half a world away in Massachusetts, Stateside. Yet these days they are married and farming oysters together happily. Fancy that eh? They run a business called NZ Native Fisheries on the Karikari Peninsula between Rangaunu Harbour and Doubtless Bay, and their oysters are exported all around the world. If you're lucky enough you may find them in a New World or PAK'nSAVE supermarket somewhere around the country, and if you do then stick them in your trolley immediately. You won't be disappointed, believe me.

Ben is a member of the Kaitaia Four Wheel Drive Club and decided it'd be fun to take his 2001 Toyota Land Cruiser 78 Series, the troop carrier version, to catch up with us in the new FJ Cruiser and show us a few of the local trails. Ben's Yankee accent is still there, but his language is that of a fair dinkum Kiwi. **His old man was an architect and came down to work on some exciting projects and developments in the area and Ben came with him. That was in 1995. He has never left.** About ten years ago he met Marara when they were working together; one thing led to another, and that was that, as they say!

DAY TWO
22 February 2011

The start of the second day saw an eager Ian and a mate of his, Luke, taking us back onto the coast and up to Pouto Point where we would test the ability of the FJ in soft sand dunes. One thing I could report after the first two days is that the FJ Cruiser likes sand.

We conquered a fifty-metre, forty-five-degree sand dune and managed to get the FJ off the ground on a few occasions, all of which was taken in its stride. Later we saw a seal, who gave us a filthy look for disturbing his peace before belching and barking and slipping into the surf.

Having left Dargaville we made our way south over farm tracks and dirt back-roads with the target of Giltrap City Toyota in central Auckland, who were hosting our first checkpoint function. There was one point where we managed to negotiate the Cruiser up and down a track that the locals reckoned only tractors could handle. The dunes were enormous, and apparently a lot softer and more difficult to traverse as there had been a lack of westerly winds to pack the sand down. So

Conquering the sand dune at Pouto Point.

Crunch!

much so that Captain Trunky, our support vehicle, got stuck (not for the last time!) and old Ian had to pull her out. But the terrain was awesome and it is here that I first got my FJ totally airborne with all four feet far from the ground. When we finally stopped for a breather, I was informed that some rooster had challenged me to wear a bra at the Puhoi Pub as the next tarseal credit. It was either that or play paintball warfare against a local posse.

DARGAVILLE TO AUCKLAND

Taking some air.

On the sand.

Testing it out in the dunes.

There's nothing worse than the support vehicle driven by an expert technician and four-wheel-driver getting stuck — nice one, Jared!

It was at that stage that I had a 'eureka' moment. That we should write a book about the classic, top-notch folk we were meeting while undertaking some of the most extraordinary motoring feats in some of the most stunning landscapes in the world. The fruit of which you have in your very hand right now.

But our delight at what we had achieved and experienced over the previous day and a half quickly turned to dismay and disbelief. As we swung into Puhoi we heard of the tragic events unfolding in Christchurch and headed to the Puhoi Pub to gauge the extent of the devastation. A 6.3-magnitude earthquake had struck the Canterbury region, centred near Christchurch, with widespread destruction and serious damage. The gravity and significance of the event really hit home when we heard John Key state that 'This day may well be New Zealand's darkest.' It most certainly was.

My mood and that of the crew had turned 180 degrees and our hearts and minds could only be with the people of Christchurch. And so clearly the Top to Bottom needed to be parked for a while — and the team at Toyota New Zealand were quick to make that decision when we all met at the Langham Hotel in Auckland.

We attended a very sombre function at Giltrap's and announced the intention to postpone the event indefinitely. Everyone fully understood and totally supported the decision. It was a horrible evening in Auckland. The rain was persisting down and the atmosphere was one of shock and sadness. The good folk at Giltrap City Toyota put on a brave face and a good show under the circumstances and after the event asked us up for a beer in the boardroom while we watched coverage of the catastrophe in Christchurch.

And so with just two days under our belt and having made it only as far as Auckland, the Top to Bottom was put on ice.

Struck by the news of the Canterbury earthquake on 22 February.

Watching events unfold.

Giltrap Toyota checkpoint.

Lee from ZM who followed us from top to bottom in Black Thunder, ZM's FJ Cruiser.

IAN RUSSELL

Now Ian Russell must be a bloody legend. He is a second cousin of mine, for goodness' sake. In fact my grandparents were his uncle and aunt, if that makes sense, and so I think that warrants second-cousin status. And you can tell we're related too. When we first caught up he took me aside and played a nasty little trick on me. We'd actually crossed paths a few years back and he reminded me of that and said he had something he'd been meaning to tell me. He ushered me away from the rest of the crew and said, **'Look, Marc, there's something I need to tell you and it may come as somewhat of a surprise — I'm your illegitimate half-brother ... '** All sorts of thoughts flashed through my mind for the second or so that passed until he burst out laughing and told me he was joking. For an instant, I fell for it hook, line and sinker. Bugger! And get this? He is also a cousin of Luke Farmer, Toyota's account manager from Saatchi & Saatchi who is a top bloke and accompanied us on the Top to Bottom trip.

At any rate, in an earlier life Ian shaped and made surfboards at Whangamata. On a surf safari to the wild north-west coast thirty or so years back, he and a mate came out of the waves and, on seeing a local cocky feeding out, offered to help. **Ian has been there ever since. From surfing (which he still does a lot of — in fact he keeps a board in a secret spot where his farm meets the sea and takes it out for a surf when time allows) to being a farmhand and to eventually being one of the largest private farmers in the country has been a fun ride for Ian, but not without its fair share of hard work.**

These days he owns and manages a couple of farms in Northland including one on the east coast over by Ngunguru — close to Sandy Bay for a surf of course. But he spends most of his time at Pouto Point. **He met us with his double-cab Hilux, which he's had for a while, and it's never given him even a spot of bother he reckons. He's always been a Toyota man.** And my word, does he know how to drive them! Some of the crew reckon we hit the ton coming down Baylys Beach — that's over 160 kilometres an hour. And thank the good Lord that we were running short of time because after he made us plunge fifty metres down a forty-five-degree slope he showed us a higher and steeper one to which he planned to take us. That we needed to keep moving en route was our excuse.

I plan on catching up with Ian again. Our family have a particular sense of humour that he certainly shares.

IN THE INTERIM

Well, there were almost three long months between the fateful 22 February and the day we finally got back on the road, 15 May. Agustina's and my second child was born only a few days after we decided to halt the journey, so it was actually fortunate that I was in Auckland at the time and not tussling with the Taranaki tussock as was planned for that day. While premature, Tomás was born a healthy little bloke, and it was great to see his little set of clangers on delivery — now Sofia has a little brother to hang with.

Meanwhile, the highlights of the first two days of the Top to Bottom Challenge made their way around the world pretty swiftly. They made it to Japan and to the Godfather of the FJ Cruiser, Mr Nishimura. Now Mr Nishimura wasn't too impressed with the way I had been treating the vehicle and decided to make a dedicated trip to New Zealand to teach me a lesson. He reckons I was going too soft on it! He designed it, he knows every inch of it and he needed to give me a serious lesson in off-road vehiculation. Mr Nishimura's English was only a shade better than my non-existent Japanese, so for the twenty minutes or so he threw the FJ Cruiser around some pretty tricky topography we just laughed in unison. He had quite a contagious cackle which kept me chortling away. And he only knew one speed at which to travel — fast, regardless of the lie of the land he was approaching. He was such a funny fulla I'd love to have taken him with me on the whole trip just to keep my spirits up were my bottom lip to drop at any stage.

Mr Nishimura.

A week or so later I took the Top to Bottom FJ Cruiser out to visit John Pickford and the team at Counties Toyota. Also present was Tony from Tuakau, one of the first FJ Cruiser customers in the country. I was lucky enough to present him with his keys. What a bloody character he was. He has recently retired from the Glenbrook Steel Mill and for years in his spare time cut and sold firewood. Now he does it more or less full time, turning the good folk of Pukekohe and surrounds' wood into firewood for their fireplaces. 'I've got the best goddamned firewood in the country,' he proudly declared. To see if he's true to his word, I plan on heading down to see him once the journey's over to pick up some of his prime manuka. I offered to pay him in Speight's but he told me politely to keep my Speight's down in Otago.

Tony was pretty stoked with John and the team at Counties Toyota, though. He told me he holds them in the highest regard, and can't thank them enough for putting on such a good show the day I popped in to hand over the keys to his brand spanking new sun-fusion-coloured FJ Cruiser. It would appear karma may have taken place. On retiring from the steel mill, Tony had decided to pop in to the local wholesaler and shout his good mates at work a few beers for the last time. At the same time, he thought it appropriate to buy a Lotto ticket. It just goes to show that the world rewards good bastards and that particular Saturday Tony became $200,000 richer!

Tony gave us some supplies for the trip that were much appreciated.

The team at Counties Toyota.

Seriously, though, it had been a quick but difficult decision to halt the journey on 22 February. I had met with Neeraj Lala, the GM for Marketing at Toyota, that fateful afternoon, together with the other marketing partners Saatchi & Saatchi and Aim Proximity Wellington. We realized that everybody's combined focus needed to be on Christchurch so the Top to Bottom project was put on hold immediately. But starting the challenge again was even bloody harder! There were all sorts of considerations, but Neeraj and I thought long and hard about it and renamed the challenge 'Top to Bottom — it just got harder'. That made us even more determined to crack it!

Via www.toptobottom.co.nz we also got some great new suggestions for what to pack given that we were likely to now be on the receiving end of some fairly inclement weather. Many suggested Icebreaker base layers, Swanndris and Swazi gear, although Kevin suggested that as a serial nudist I just crank up the heater in the FJ to keep myself toasty, as the weight of clothes would only increase the fuel bill. Mike suggested a dog as a companion so it could clean up the dropped pies and fallen debris from snacking while driving. Briar quite sensibly suggested a spare set of keys for the truck. One young damsel even volunteered to be a winch-wench, and while the idea was very plausible I found the terminology slightly derogatory and offensive.

I got several sensible suggestions to slip some steak-and-cheese pies, wrapped in tinfoil, under the bonnet on the manifold to heat them up. Commonly known as car-cooking.

There was no end of recommendations for legendary lads and ladies to meet up with (there was one bloke who owned eight Land Cruisers, which is quite extraordinary, if a tad greedy) and trails to trial, many of which we incorporated into the itinerary.

Another bonus was that BP turned up to the party. They generously donated some petrol vouchers to help us get from top to bottom in the Beast and Captain Trunky. It was highly appreciated and an endorsement of the strength, value and reach of the project.

And just to reiterate. As if the challenge wasn't tough enough, and now with the added element of risk due to the elements, the hooers at Toyota made a deal that I needed to undertake more tests in order to earn credits to drive on the tarseal. Some of the ideas put forward were nothing short of sadistic!

But I couldn't wait to get back on the road, continue the challenge and meet the good bastards who were to come out of the woodwork. Because we were off the beaten track, the people appeared more interesting and interested. Some of them fed us, some of them housed us, but all of them entertained us. Every one of them had a story to tell, so we've included a few of them.

Mr Nishimura puts the FJ Cruiser to the test.

DAY THREE
15 May 2011

So back into it we were. The crew assembled and headed to where it was all about to begin again. The legendary Puhoi Pub was the start line.

It's fitting that the Puhoi Pub has become one of the most historical pubs in the southern hemisphere given that the chaps who built it and first drank beer from its taps were from near Pilsen in Bohemia (today the Czech Republic), home of the refreshing Pilsener beer. In 1863, after one hell of a journey to get there and promised fertile land they were dumped in Puhoi and left isolated. The pub has been the focal point of the Bohemian community there ever since and is replete with relics of bygone eras. Now it's a popular stopover for many heading north out of Auckland and a beloved destination in its own right.

Quite a crowd had gathered there to see the FJ too. A fulla called Mike Stearne had the great idea that I should serve a few of the thirsty patrons an ale. Initially, we thought that an absurd idea as we were leaving at 10.30 a.m. But as sure as God made little apples there were a few blokes wanting to get on the sauce even at that hour. I had no issue whatsoever with serving them. What I was not so comfortable with was pouring them a blisteringly cold pint, delivering it to them and then having to watch them drink it as I was about to drive for nigh on twelve hours. Anyway, the lucky recipient was a strawberry blond (a term that I have always battled to understand to be frank — to me it's like saying a banana redhead) whose mate reckoned it must have been 'buy a ginga a beer day'. Like a true blue ginga, he appeared to savour every sip. I was later told he owned three FJ40s. Quite an enthusiast indeed!

We left the rather large legion who had assembled at the pub and pointed the FJ in the direction of Port Waikato, although a few hard core four-wheel-drivers like Ron in his FJ40, complete with a 350 Chev, tagged along. We hit some trails until we came across Delta Force Paintball Park in the middle of the Woodhill Forest near Helensville. By coincidence I thought. But by design it was, as I later found out. The crew had decided that pouring pints was hardly a demanding enough challenge to warrant tarseal credits so had a nasty little surprise in store for me. To be able to pass through Auckland (where there is little choice but to spend some time on the road) I had to take the Triple T. That stands for ten shots and ten paces and topless.

The build-up was intense. I had to wait until a group about to play was being briefed. I was visibly a tad nervous, particularly when the instructor was warning the group against not being well covered and shooting too close to an opponent. Step up Jared Burns, part of the crew, a support driver from Toyota, for his day in the sun. He had a few practice rounds to get his eye in then took aim at point-blank range. Well, bugger me! He must be a sharpshooting marksman in his spare time 'cause he bloody well hit me nine times out of ten. It was all over in about five smoking seconds. The bleeding was almost instant, the welts came later. I tried to contain the yelping and sprinted around in an attempt to distract myself from the severe sting. The yellow paint mixed with the red blood and for a while my back was covered in an orange gooey substance.

TOP TO BOTTOM:
Jared loads his weapon.
Jared lands his first shot.
His second shot hits exactly the same spot as the first.
Bullet wounds.
Bullet hole.

PUHOI
TO
PORT WAIKATO

LIVING LEGENDS

RON HARLAND

Ron Harland is a contractor from Kaukapakapa and a foundation member of the Rodney Four Wheel Drive Club. He just loves playing in the mud. He organizes tours for the club, which now has over thirty members. They've recently just been around the bottom of the North Island off-road.

Ron's got a lovely 1985 FJ70 with a 350 cubic inch Chevy engine. It comes with a rear-mounted radiator and most modifications you need to do some serious off-roading. He's also got an 80 Series Land Cruiser as a daily drive.

Ron met us at the Puhoi Pub with others from the Rodney Club, including his mate Steve Sagar, who owns — get this — an FJ70, an FJ45 with a 6.2-litre V8 diesel, and a Hilux racing truck with a supercharged V8! Ron was only planning on wishing us farewell, but the crew and I managed to persuade him and Steve to come through to the Jeep Woodhill 4WD Adventure Park. They did.

After some adventurous driving in the mud, including leading me through the bog, where I managed to get stuck, poor Ron then somehow managed to put his FJ70 arse over kite. Remarkably, when we rolled it back onto its wheels, the only damage was a small crack in the windscreen.

When Charlie and I caught up with Ron a month later he said apart from replacing the windscreen, he didn't need to do anything to it and that it's running like a charm. He also told us he was awarded a little prize at the Rodney Four Wheel Drive Club monthly meeting. He was presented a box that contained a whole lot of toilet paper with a Picnic chocolate bar placed on it — doesn't take much to imagine what that resembled, with a message reading, **'When your Bottom points to the sky, it's not a Top day.'**

I reckon Ron will remember Top to Bottom for a long time!

MATT CARNELL

Matt Carnell is a lovely bloke. He's a very keen member of the Rodney Off Road Club. He came from Red Beach to Puhoi to wish us well on our merry way for the restart of the Top to Bottom Challenge. He turned up with his son Ethan in his wife Victoria's 80 Series Land Cruiser. Matt's owned six Land Cruisers in his time and has two 40 Series in his garage that slowly but surely he's restoring. One of them he's 'monster-trucking' with forty-inch tyres, 80-Series diffs and everything big. Having said that, he's kept the original six-cylinder engine in it. Then he's building a hot rod street version, which he's popped a Lexus V8 into to really pimp it out.

The competition.

But there was no time for self-pity. My shirt was back on and I was in the truck and through the Jeep Woodhill 4WD Adventure Park. Given the bumpy ride, I feared the chafing on the welts from the back of my seat would turn them gangrenous. Luckily, my mind had to be focused on other things at hand.

Like negotiating some pretty tricky tracks, which I managed to do reasonably well. To say the weather was inclement would be understating things and to say that the tracks were not for the faint-hearted would be totally extracting the urine. This was testing even for seasoned four-wheel-drivers.

It was all going well until I just couldn't resist heading straight into a mud pool that I was told to steer clear of. The inevitable happened.

I was donkey deep in a pool of mud. I couldn't even open the door. The initial option was to be pulled out by another Land Cruiser, but the crew from Jeep Woodhill 4WD Adventure Park coached us through self-winching the FJ out of the deep by anchoring to a tree and using leverage. Given the lie of the land we had to stop and use different trees to get us in the directions we needed to go.

Not long after I'd pulled myself out of the massive mud hole, an apparition appeared. Over the horizon and through the gate came a fully pimped-out purple 1976 FJ40 with two smoking hot babes and a bag full of burgers. Just what the doctor ordered. The good folk at BurgerFuel had kindly delivered us a couple of bags stacked full of their iconic Chicken Backfire and Bastard Beef Burgers. They went down an absolute treat! Thanks, BurgerFuel.

But before we could let our digestive systems get into their stride we were back into our work.

Bugger!

A near deadly descent followed and one of the locals, Ron from Rodney, who'd followed us from Puhoi, got a bit overexcited and rolled his Land Cruiser on its roof after it slid back down a steep incline and nudged off a tree at the wrong angle. Fortunately, there was no damage to the owner or the vehicle, which after being winched the right way up, started first pop and was off like a shot. I must admit to feeling a pang of guilt, given we'd talked Ron into joining us, when all he had initially planned to do was wave us on our merry way from Puhoi.

Ron goes on his roof.

Dave to the rescue. A mysterious man — I don't know if I ever saw his eyes.

LIVING LEGENDS

ROGER WINSLADE

Roger Winslade was such a four-wheel-drive enthusiast that he decided to start the best 4x4 park in Auckland! He took his inspiration from friend Graeme Sinclair, of TV show *Gone Fishin'* fame, a truly inspirational man, who has led a life in the outdoors hunting and fishing, written several books and lives a remarkable life regardless of some setbacks life's thrown back at him. Roger discussed with Graeme his plans to open a four-

wheel-drive park and Graeme told him to just go for it. And it's the best thing he ever did. He organizes day trips, family trips, night trips and competitions at the only venue in Auckland specifically designed for four-wheel-drivers — the Jeep Woodhill 4WD Adventure Park. While he was hosting us, as we cut through his park on Day Three, he told me he just gets a real kick out of people coming to have a good time at his park, especially the first timers who get a taste for more.

DAVE STEVENS

You can tell just by the photo that Dave Stevens knows what the hell he's doing. Not only is he an ardent member of the Auckland Land Rover Owners Club in his spare time (even though he's just sold his Land Rover and bought a Nissan Patrol) and helps out with recovery work at the Jeep Woodhill 4WD Adventure Park, his day job is the supervision and piloting of oversized loads, such as houses and heavy machinery.

He was just the man we needed then, when I got a bit over-enthusiastic and tried to sail the Beast through a lake ...

Jeep Woodhill 4WD Adventure Park.

It would be really uncool to destroy the FJ on our first day back.

Trusty Captain Trunky, never far behind.

Moss leading the charge.

Dave lends a hand again.

On the way to Auckland.

Also with us was Moss Burmester, the Commonwealth Games record holder for the 200-metres butterfly and 2008 World Champion of the same event. He and his girlfriend Melissa are keen off-roaders and were excellent company on the trying tracks through Woodhill Forest.

After some more tricky moments negotiating the clay, some more obstacles, hills and creeks, and temporarily losing the tyre from its rim, we powered through Auckland and headed to Limestone Downs.

It's amazing what these trucks can do and where they can go.

LIVING LEGENDS

MOSS BURMESTER

Moss Burmester really is a legend. A 2006 Commonwealth Games gold medal and World Champion in 2008, both for the 200-metres butterfly, is proof of that! But did you know he's a budding four-wheel-driver too?

It's one of his latest passions — quite a good fit given his love of the outdoors and his interest in boys' toys. He's currently running a 1985 FJ70 Series Toyota Land Cruiser and he and his girlfriend Melissa were great company as we tackled the West Auckland wilderness.

Alf, Pam and Chris treated us to a fine feast.

Limestone Downs is an 8000-acre farm owned by a charitable trust. It was initially owned by a very generous bloke by the name of Charles Almer Baxter. Charles was a remarkable joker. He was born in Otago in 1857 and later trained as a land surveyor. He then made his fortune in Malaya, surveying and tin mining. After he returned to New Zealand, he bought Limestone Downs and after his death it was to provide for his only daughter. When she later passed on with no children, the trust was set up and the income from Limestone Downs goes to provide for agricultural science and education.

The locals at Limestone Downs were generous buggers, all pitching in a plate, and we ate like kings. Chris and Pam Barber were our hosts for the night and we ate our way through some fine wild pork and lamb chops in addition to standard barbecue fare. Poor old Chris had recently lopped the end of his thumb off. He was chopping up the dog tucker and the end of his thumb ended up being a bit extra for the dog's dinner. All in a day's work, but that didn't stop him turning the meat on the barbie to perfection that night. Chris and Pam, and Alf Harwood, the farm manager, looked after us brilliantly. The team here put on a pot-luck dinner and Chris told us how good the fishing off the coast of the farm was.

So after a long and satisfying feed, we hit the hay in the shearers' quarters for some well overdue shut-eye.

LIVING LEGENDS

KATIE DU FALL AND FARRELL JAKOBI

Katie du Fall and her good friend Farrell Jakobi, the two BurgerFuel foxes who brought out us some super sustenance on Day Three, were great sports indeed. They had to drive in the persisting rain and ferocious winds from the BurgerFuel store in Henderson all the way to Woodhill Forest — topless. Well the car was topless, not them — sadly. But it was a splendid effort on their part, no

less, because the weather was anything but pretty. I had begun to wonder what we were going to eat given that we were stuck in the middle of the sticks and I could have eaten the crutch out of a low-flying duck I was so hungry. So when these two lasses arrived with big smiles and big burgers it was a welcome surprise. The crew were also ravenous so when Katie and Farrell turned up with a couple of bags of burgers they were pretty damn stoked.

Katie was born in Rotorua, came up to Auckland to study a Bachelor of Communications, and then landed a job in the BurgerFuel marketing department where she still works today and loves every minute of it. Katie's ideal partner in crime on a mission like this, Farrell, is on the other hand South African born, although she's been here since she was eight, and when she's not studying at university helps out BurgerFuel with promotional work.

The co-CEOs of BurgerFuel, Josef Roberts and Chris Mason, have quite a stable of classic cars in addition to the 1976 FJ40 the girls turned up in, the favourite of mine being a 1974, 265-Hemi, Chrysler Valiant Charger. Josef bought the FJ40 in Australia quite a few years back and has been working on it ever since. It comes decked out with a 350-cubic-inch, four-barrel V8 that has a nice throaty rumble to it. The interior is white leather and it's got a raft of other custom fittings. Rumours are that it now has the number plate EAT ME.

BurgerFuel is a true Kiwi sensation — their motto is 'engineering the ultimate burger experience' and that they certainly do. The fact the Saudi Arabians and Iraqis are all over their burgers like a rash just goes to show their rock star status on the world stage. 'Death Before Bad Burgers' they say, and you can't really argue with that.

DAY FOUR
16 May 2011

Once again we were up well before sparrow's fart. Even in the early-morning darkness we could tell the weather gods were out to test our mettle on Day Four.

We were caught in a wicked weather bomb at Port Waikato. It had turned fairly ugly, to say the least, with horizontal rain lashing hard. It was the windy west coast at its most wild. There was a TVNZ cross for the *Breakfast* show and our old mate Tony, who I'd met at Counties Toyota a month or so back, turned up in his new FJ Cruiser waxing lyrical and bearing some greats gifts for us, to make the trip more enjoyable. Thanks, Tony!

We met up again with the manager of Limestone Downs, Alf Harwood. Alf had been our host the night prior with Chris and Pam and was to point us in the right direction to Raglan. He sort of did that. 'Follow that slippery track there all the way to the coast' were his exact words if I recall well.

So you can imagine our jubilation (read frustration) when we finally slid our way to the coast only to find the storm had pushed the tide up and there was no way in the world we could cross the beach and the tidal stream — it was far too dangerous to attempt. A friendly Welsh farmhand called Steve Rees told us in no uncertain terms we were shit out of luck and we had to turn back. Well, I can tell you getting back up the boggy, slippery slope was a damn sight harder than coming down it. It needed full concentration. Good job the young Welshman followed us in his tractor. The weather conditions could only be described as extreme. But, once again, the FJ rose to the challenge.

Anne, Phil and the Nikau Cave and Café.

We needed to replenish so we headed to Nikau Cave and Café. The café is bordered on three sides by a stream and sits below steep green hills that are full of protruding limestone. We sat down at a big macrocarpa table and had a graze, graciously hosted by Anne and Phil Woodward. It was all pretty pleasant — yet what awaited me wasn't.

This tarseal challenge was the hardest yet. For me at least — I suffer from horrific claustrophobia and someone had had the smart idea that to be able to get on the road to fill up with gas I needed to traverse a full kilometre under the ground! And not just under the ground, but in a cave that, in places, is really only big enough for wetas, glow-worms and eels. If I knew just how tight things were going to get in there I would never have done it. I had to sandwich myself down a bloody crevasse and then crawl along an underground stream. It was terrifying.

I'd rather have been buried alive in a coffin, to be perfectly frank. The guide, at one stage, pointed out some stalactites and stalagmites but buggered if I was interested in those. I had one thing on my mind and that was to get the flock out of there. Eighty long terrifying minutes later I was through — and just quietly pretty chuffed with myself. Sometimes you've just got to look fear in the face and charge on through it.

PORT WAIKATO TO RAGLAN

OPPOSITE PAGE: A happy Welshman, Steve Rees.

LIVING LEGENDS

ALF HARWOOD

Alf Harwood manages the farm at Limestone Downs. All 8000 acres of it! It's owned by a charitable trust and runs sheep and beef. Alf came to Limestone Downs as head shepherd in 1968 and has now been managing the farm for over ten years. **He drives a Toyota Land Cruiser as his daily drive but wasn't that keen on getting it dirty the day we were there.** He's got a Nissan for the farm work.

With the proceeds of the trust, Alf hosts British farmers out to Limestone Downs to further their education. They've had over a hundred out since Alf's been managing the farm. Steve Rees, the big Welsh bloke who guided us in his tractor, is one of them. Alf and Chris and Pam Barber really treated us to a feast the night we stayed at Limestone Downs in Port Waikato.

ANNE AND PHIL WOODWARD

Initially, there was no way I was able to say that Phil was a really decent bloke — **he was the bastard who suggested I do the entire Nikau Cave as a tarseal challenge.** Halfway through I wanted to throttle him such was the anxiety I was feeling at being in a rat-hole, deep underground. But the jubilation of making it through after an hour and a half and the thrill of seeing limestone formations and caverns full of glow-worms outweighed the discomfort. So, yes, Phil is a good bugger. He has been shearing sheep for forty years and still does. But he's also been commercial caving for nearly twenty. Cool jobs.

And Anne, his wife, is lovely too. She was a nurse and married Phil in 1975. Five kids and many years later she opened the Nikau Cave and Café. She loves cooking and gardening and does both for the café. Go and check it out. You'll be impressed.

No one can enjoy this, surely.

I surfaced, wet, muddy and still shaking, but successful — and was promptly met by Phil and Anne's daughter, Emily Welch, who holds the record for (if you can believe this) shearing 648 sheep in one day! That's the most by a female ever. Quite an outstanding record. In actual fact she sheared 650 sheep but two were disqualified on a technicality — something about not being completely crutched. She joined us in the FJ and took us up to the woolshed to talk us through her prowess with some shears. Nowadays she manages a shearing gang and two young kids. Gutsy stuff indeed.

Strange but beautiful things happen when you're a kilometre underground.

EMILY WELCH

A true living legend, Emily Welch holds the women's nine-hour lamb-shearing world record. **No sheila on the planet has shorn more lambs in that time.** Pretty impressive, eh? But she's really down to earth and has no tickets on herself despite being the fastest female shearer ever!

It's a good thing that she puts her talents to good use then. She runs a shearing contract business with nine shearers and nine shed staff. It was a natural progression from being a shearer to starting her own business. She and her husband, Sam, also lease 250 acres from Emily's olds, Phil and Anne Woodward, where they farm Coopworth sheep. On top of all that, Emily is a mother to two young children.

Emily and Sam live on twenty-one acres near Waikaretu and are the proud owners of an old sky-blue Hilux Surf. Sam feels a little bit upstaged by his good wife, so is attempting to break a record himself. He's having a crack at the blokes' two-man team nine-hour ewe record of 1335 ewes. Good luck to him!

A tour of the shearing shed.

Next stop was at Tom Mandeno's farm. Tom's got a beaut Land Cruiser and actually has his original one, that's been a family heirloom for years, in the hay shed for spare parts. Tom insisted that the crew and I pop into his digs for some liquid refreshments, an offer we gladly accepted. There we shot the breeze with Tom, his wife Anna and his daughter Kate for the thick end of an hour.

From there it was back on track to Raglan, and my horribly hard-earned tarseal credits were redeemed on a slim stretch of road on the way into the town, twelve hours after we had left Port Waikato.

We laid our weary heads down at Dominique's Bow Street Studios in Raglan, with magnificent views of the Whaingaroa Harbour, framed by a couple of majestic pohutukawas, and went out with the lights.

Tom's 'new' Land Cruiser.

LIVING LEGENDS

TOM MANDENO

Tom Mandeno is the quintessential Kiwi cocky. Loyal to a fault, as honest as the day is long, generous, genuine and just a salt-of-the-earth good bloke. Well, that's certainly the impression I got after spending an hour or so with him. Tom's farm, which he bought in 1973, borders that of Phil and Anne Woodward of Nikau Cave and Café fame. Phil and Anne suggested that we pop up and see Tom and that cutting across his farm would be a nice short cut. So we did just that. But as a true man of the land he had to ask us in to rehydrate and have a little snack. After a brutally long day driving up hill and down dale, a relaxing chat with Tom, his wife Anna and daughter Kate, was just what the doctor ordered.

Tom inherited a Land Rover as part of the settlement of the farm, which he used for three years or so. In 1976, the government of the day announced that farmers could claim forty per cent of the capital expenditure of farm equipment as an expense, and then depreciate a further twenty-five per cent of the asset every year, effectively meaning you could expense sixty-five per cent of a farm vehicle in the first year. So Tom went into Lockyer Motors in Pukekohe and bought a brand-spanking-new Toyota Land Cruiser FJ40. This original Land Cruiser gave him thirty years of sterling service until 2006 when after a long, hard life Tom retired it. But it still sits in his hay shed and serves as an organ donor for his 'young' Land Cruiser that he now uses on the farm, a 1978 FJ40 he bought when he felt his original one finally needed a rest.

Like so many of the legends we met on this trip, Tom and his family wished us well and told us we could pop in again anytime for a cup of tea and a natter and that next time we should stay for dinner.

DAY FIVE
17 May 2011

The next morning was another early-bird start and we left the mighty Waikato headed for New Plymouth.

For some ungodly reason we were going via Te Kuiti. Not that I have anything against Te Kuiti by any stretch of the imagination, but it appeared to me to be a bit wayward and off-track. Apparently, a short cut was up through a quarry, but after a pretty hair-raising ride beside a sheer drop (where I had my seatbelt unfastened and my hands poised to propel me out of danger should the Beast tip over the edge), and another twenty minutes of dirt track, when we reached the top we realized that all we had done was add considerable time to our journey.

Why not go up through a quarry?

Some short cut!

Now where do we go?

RAGLAN
TO
NEW PLYMOUTH

The good old Haddad boys.

Tasman Toyota checkpoint.

A nutritious hot dog hand-delivered by Kees.

Ploughing through Carl and Sonia Hurley's farm.

A highly worthwhile stop was Haddad's Menswear in Otorohanga, a recommendation by Simon Gilbert via the Top to Bottom website, and a simply sensational suggestion indeed. The Haddad brothers were very dapperly dressed, as apparently they always are. I had actually been in the store many years ago and they still had a photo of us together. Unfortunately, I was looking a few years younger in the photo than now, but these blokes hadn't changed one iota.

They fitted me out in the full-monty Swanndri and a woolly-eared hat and sent us on our way. From Otorohanga we headed for Te Kuiti via tracks. There we caught up with Carl and Sonia Hurley. Carl was one of the first owners of the new FJ Cruiser in New Zealand. Not long prior to us coming through he'd been out the back of his brother's place following his motorbike up such a steep gradient that the dogs were falling off the back, and he got right to the top of the hill in his FJ with just standard road tyres on it!

Carl led us out on a quad with Sonia on horseback, and you'd have to say, judging by the ease with which she was handling the track we were on, that a horse is a pretty bloody good way around a farm.

After more treacherous terrain we made it to New Plymouth. And we had a brilliant turnout at Tasman Toyota. It was all on for young and old. Five-year-old Kees brought me a much appreciated snarler in bread with plenty of tomato sauce, and there was an FJ colouring-in competition for the kids. A great show indeed. I think the party lasted for about three hours.

LIVING LEGENDS

KARAM AND JOHN HADDAD

It's hard to get a word in edgewise when you're around John and Karam Haddad, the couple of absolute bloody characters who own and run Haddad's Menswear in Otorohanga.

John and Karam, **two old-school thrumpets and fair dinkum Kiwis,** are the sons of the local fruiterer, who about seventy-five years ago opened Michael's Milkbar, one of the original milkbars in the country, which the Haddad boys still own today.

In 1965 Karam opened Haddad's Menswear, next door to Michael's Milkbar, and John joined him in 1971. They pride themselves on serving the customer with the best quality at the best price — and proof they are doing their job is their huge and loyal customer base who act as Haddad's ambassadors and make referrals. They sell the top brands and wherever possible support New Zealand made and New Zealand companies and teams such as Swazi, Swanndri and the All Blacks. Their constituency there in the northern King Country is the rural community, mainly dry stock and dairy farmers. **So they have all forms of outdoor wear and footwear including their own brands for the ladies:** Haddad's Bush Babes — Protecting New Zealand's Assets; Haddad's Beach Babes — Proceed With Caution; Haddad's V8 Babes — Awesome Power; Haddad's Farm Babes — New Zealand's Greatest Assets.

They're on State Highway 3 on the main road so they also get all sorts of people popping in, including tourists heading south from Waitomo and those ski bunnies driving past to get to Mt Ruapehu. And they love it! Their life is in the shop. There's nowhere else they'd want to be. In fact when they're not there all they can think about are all the people they are missing. John drives a Chevy pick-up, which he bought new in 1984, and as an example of how little they like leaving Otorohanga, it has done less than 60,000 kilometres. He's also got his dad Michael's old Pontiac Laurentian stored in the garage.

The Haddad boys had been following the Top to Bottom Challenge but had no idea we were coming in. They treated us brilliantly, together with Wendy from the store. And talked non-stop the whole time we were there. They kitted me out top to bottom. Well, almost. After we'd left, they realized they'd forgotten the 'bottom'. So would you believe it, **they couriered two pairs of their legendary 'built in fatigue protection' socks all the way to Christchurch and they were waiting for us when we got there! Legends!**

SEAN COLES

Sean Coles is a construction manager who was in the process of recon-structing a big slip by putting a road on top of it when we rocked up and asked if we could take a short cut up through a quarry. Sean was very obliging.

Originally from Blighty, he now lives in Hororata, near Darfield in Canterbury, and has been there for four and a half years, although recently he's been working for Transfield Services in the West Waikato, doing all sorts of roading and infrastructure work, including adding all the safety features like barriers and cat's-eyes and what have you.

Hailing from Cambridge in Britain, he and his family then lived in France before moving to New Zealand. And he's never going back to England, he reckons — he's now a die-hard fan of the All Blacks, as is his son Ethan, who plays in the Darfield under 10s, and his daughter Sophie. For a Pom, Sean was a damn good joker!

SONIA AND CARL HURLEY

There's no time for Sonia and Carl Hurley to get sick because they both work seven days a week. Well, Sonia does anyway; occasionally Carl sneaks off for a fish. He's a keen fisherman and recently came second in a jet-ski fishing competition. He often goes on his jet-ski for snapper and kingfish out from Kawhia or out in the Manukau Harbour.

Most mornings they are up at 5.30 a.m. to feed the 700-odd cows they have on their Te Kuiti farm. They normally

get them at about four days old and fatten them up for about six months until they reach 100 kilograms. They can manage up to 2000 calves a year.

In spring, Carl spends all day running around picking up colostrum and Sonia spends all day running around picking up calves. It's a good job then that **they both have their truck licences and between them own two Toyota trucks and four Land Cruisers — including a stylish new FJ Cruiser! Sonia, though, is most at home on a horse**, methinks, and led us quite a distance on one.

Sonia and Carl are great people and great hosts and let us through their farm even though we tore it up a bit, given the wet conditions.

How was I going to compete with them?

I'll die trying. Wasted.

Hurt.

 But that wasn't the end of the day. Oh no. Not yet. It was down to East End Skate Rink where we had been invited and I was to be challenged for the privilege of driving out of New Plymouth via tarseal the next morning. An invitation that had come via the Taranaki Roller Corps Derby Girls. To cut a long story short, the result was me copping a beating and being totally humiliated, thumped and punished by two dozen birds on roller skates. It all ended with a melee of twenty chicks heaped on top of me hurling me insults, knees, elbows and forearms. It's put me off roller-skating for the rest of my life.

After that, there was only one remedy — a trip to the Lone Star for a ridiculously large serving of Redneck Ribs and a few cold beers to wash them down with. We ate and burped our way through a barbaric meal. One of the best ways to end a long, hard day.

Humiliated.

DAY SIX
18 May 2011

The next morning we met up with Tamati and the team at TVNZ, once again at what felt like the middle of the night.

Some of us who had over-indulged in the Lone Star ribs the night before had woken up with a meat hangover. We were positioned right on the Taranaki coast with some whopping great swells pumping in. The temperature gauge in the FJ Cruiser read 7°C, but with the wind whistling in sideways and the severe wind chill factor it felt like far below zero. At that point I was thanking my lucky stars that we'd been in to see the Haddad boys the day before to get a thick-skinned Swanndri. A fair crowd had gathered, which was a gutsy effort given the harsh weather, including a couple of the Taranaki Roller Corps Derby Girls, wearing their game-day attire and braving the elements.

Cold, wet and dark.

NEW PLYMOUTH TO RANGATAUA

Not them again, please!

In the cold light of day I realized just what powerfully built and athletic young women they were — no wonder they had humiliated me with such ease the night before. You can't play their sport if you're petite would be my synopsis!

We'd had some good tips from the locals about how to head south off-road, with most, such as Lisa Crow and Steve Horton, saying we needed to take the old Forgotten World Highway up through Whangamomona (try saying that quickly with two dry Weet-Bix in your pie-hole!). While the Beast was eating up any territory that was put in front of it, we had to change course a few times because of swollen rivers and creeks with burst banks caused by the persistent, pouring precipitation.

The Forgotten World Highway is 150 kilometres long and was built on colonial bridal paths from the late nineteenth century. It had been described to me as an upsy-downsy roller coaster through some of the most rugged and mysterious landscape in the country, including wriggling around and over four mountain saddles and along the Tangarakau Gorge, which derives its name, meaning felled trees, from those cut down by the legendary Tamatea to repair his canoes for travelling on the Whanganui River. In better weather you can see the tips of Mt Taranaki to the west and Ruapehu, Tongariro and Ngauruhoe to the east.

Not long after leaving Stratford, a fuel stop at the local BP, and a windy (as in curvy, not gusty) ride in the gravel to the heart of the Highway up to the Central Plateau, we were confronted by a colossal truck coming in the opposite direction. I gave it such a wide berth to give it some room we slipped into the roadside gutter. The crew rigged up the rope from Captain Trunky, but I decided that sometimes a bit of brute force is all that is needed and planted my hoof and turned the wheel hard and rode it out. The blokes driving the trucks hopped out for a yak and when I asked them what was the best way to get to Whangamomona they drily replied, 'Slowly.'

Oops.

As we had just found out the track was pretty narrow and, given the weather conditions, extra caution was the call for the corners. In parts the trail was no cakewalk to say the least, and as if we needed a reminder as to how remote we were we saw all number of wild goats, pigs and even a few deer. Had we been better armed we would by no means have gone hungry.

Nothing brute force wasn't going to fix.

Day Six was a magic day.

I think this is the entire school roll.

Possibly the most remote watering hole in the country.

The weather had started to improve when deep in the middle of nowhere we came across the only settlement on the way through to Taumarunui, the near ghost town of Whangamomona, in the 'Valley of the Plenty' which flourished as a coal mining village around the turn of the nineteenth century, but went into serious decline after a major flood in 1924. In 1988, after local government divided the Whangamomona district in two with half remaining in Taranaki and the other half being allocated to Manawatu, the residents of Whangamomona (who had not been consulted prior) declared Whangamomona a republic. They now celebrate its independence every second January, when over 5000 people flock there to get among good fun traditions, like gumboot throwing, sheep racing, possum skinning, lumber-jacking, whip cracking and clay-bird shooting. Given its sovereign status, I needed to pop in to visit the district authorities and get a passport, which are issued at the local historic pub. The informative publicans, Penny and Geoff Taylor, gave me a history lesson of the Republic of Whangamomona, which among its illustrious presidents has included a goat named Billy that was duly elected by the populace. Sadly, Billy died while in office. Officially, there were no suspicious circumstances surrounding his death, thank goodness. But conspiracy theories abound.

We also popped in to the local school to catch up with the fifteen kids there, which was a hoot. Good country stock they were!

Whangamomona school kids cram into the Beast.

Ah, the serenity.

Passing through the Forgotten World Highway.

After waving goodbye to the school kids we were back on the Forgotten World Highway and with the thick forest canopy and the 180-metre-long, single-lane Moki Tunnel built in 1936, we lost GPS coverage, which made a few people tracking us from Wellington a tad nervous. Just through the Moki Tunnel (wide enough for only one vehicle with no room to stick your arms out the side of the vehicle), I found a bush track which led the crew and me up to the top of a hill with some stunning views. Travelling the Forgotten World Highway, which was once home to hundreds, really was a step back in time.

We came across this house on fire. Luckily, there was no one within cooee.

What road?

When we finally arrived at Taumarunui, I wasn't in the mood for any silly tarseal challenges, so when I spied a Jilesen Contractors Kenworth truck with an empty trailer, I went over and had a quiet word to the driver, Kyle Gibbs. He kindly agreed to let me drive the FJ Cruiser up onto the tray of his twenty-two-wheeler rig and we caught a sneaky ride with him along a stretch of road. Sometimes you have to get a little creative — adversity breeds genius they reckon, and what we were about to do was not technically drive the FJ on tarseal. Brilliant thinking!

One of the locals at Owhango washing his truck.

42 Traverse Track.

We then backed her off at Owhango where a few locals were gathered to greet us, and show us the base of the 42 Traverse Track. We went through some wicked tracks there and one rooster even took us through the first stage despite the winter warnings not to enter.

Another local keen for a yak.

Getting close to Horopito.

Let's see what's up over here.

We left the locals at Owhango to enjoy a few beers and Codys among themselves and moved on. The day had begun to close in, but we needed one last stop. Smash Palace. Also known as Horopito Motor Wreckers — home to two of my favourite movie scenes out of *Smash Palace* and *Goodbye Pork Pie*. This graveyard of vehicles from the 1920s through to the 1970s covers acres and is the largest vintage vehicle dismantler in Australasia. Despite all its potential, Horopito never thrived as a town after the native bush had been felled so the school finally closed in 1966 and the post office in 1971, but Horopito Motors, founded by Bill Cole in the forties, is still fully operational and doing a roaring trade. As eerie as it is, it has a real charm and presence, especially for a classic-car bogan petrol-head like me.

Smash Palace.

I wonder how long since she's put out a fire.

Rest in peace, ladies.

The Central Plateau.

 What sounded like an easy tarseal challenge in principle, but was rather more tricky in practice, and suggested by Nigel Rawson, was in fact quite essential. The fuel light on the Beast had begun flashing, so we were in need of some gas. My challenge was to get that by hand, by myself. I knew those jerry cans I bought would come in handy. Some siphoning later, without any adverse effects, and some tarseal credits were in the bank!

By then it was too late to get through to Ngamatea, our expected destination, so we stopped just short at Rangataua, thanks to a kind offer to bunk down in an old ski bach. The whole crew was pretty keen to celebrate what had been an excellent day so we headed into Ohakune and had a graze and an ale at the Powderkeg. A superb day — but another one awaited!

TED WILLIAMSON

We arrived at Smash Palace just as it was about to close. Poor old Ted Williamson, the foreman of the yard, and a towie for Horopito Motors, thought his day was finished. Then we turned up.

But we had to have a butcher's hook around Smash Palace and Ted was such a good bloke we were keen for a yarn with him. He was only happy to oblige. Given that Horopito Motors mainly deals in vintage car parts and that people visit from all around the globe, Ted has met all sorts. He reckons the only type he hasn't met is an Eskimo. Earlier that day he'd sold a heater-box from an old Triumph to a bloke from India.

His pet project is a '48 Fordson pick-up. It's a funny little thing with a 900 cc motor in it (which apparently you can almost pick up and walk around with), but quite a cool-looking ride. His daily drive is a Hilux that in his spare time he takes hunting. Ted lives up in Pipiriki on the Whanganui River. The place has no power and Ted and his partner do all their cooking on a coal range (or the barbie). No electricity, but he does have a jet-boat. Quite a lifestyle!

LIVING LEGENDS

PENNY AND GEOFF TAYLOR

Geoff and Penny Taylor consider themselves Cantabrians. Neither was born there, but they have spent more time there than anywhere else in their interesting lives. They were travelling though the Forgotten World Highway, checking it out as a motorcycle route, when they stopped for some sustenance and rehydration at the Whangamomona Hotel. A very small notice advising that the pub was for sale caught Penny's eye. She and Geoff decided to enquire, purely out of curiosity, to see what buying a pub involved and how much it would cost. They had no initial intention to buy it whatsoever. But slowly their intrigue turned to desire, and they figured this would be a great next challenge in their journey together.

That was four years ago, and they thoroughly love what they do. They reckon you never quite know who is going to walk into the pub such is the cross-section of eclectic human beings that come through the front door. They get people from all spectrums of society. Fascinating considering it's allegedly the most remote country pub in the nation. Whangamomona village has a population of thirteen, but there are about 120 people in the catchment area, which is about a half-hour drive in any direction.

They live above the bar, and as a result the place has a very homely feel to it. When there are few people in the bar it's a bit like being in Geoff and Penny's living room. They try to mix service and a friendly welcome into one. In a reflection of today's egalitarian society, Penny's predominantly the publican and Geoff does the cooking. It's genuine country hospitality in there — and it's a real shame we couldn't have settled in for a session with the locals and stayed the night. Apparently, the accommodation is first rate too!

LIVING LEGENDS

KYLE GIBBS

Kyle is a lovely fulla, born and bred in Taumarunui, where he's lived for most of his life. **Like most young kids, Kyle dreamed of motorcycles and trucks.** So after returning to Taumarunui from boarding school, he set about doing his motorbike mechanic apprenticeship and worked on super-bikes for none other than New Zealand F1 champion Russell Josiah for about six years. He even met the legendary John Britten, who designed a speed-record-breaking bike with innovative design features still way ahead of contemporary design.

For the last fifteen years, Kyle has been working as a contract truckie for Jilesen Contractors and loves every minute of it. He gets to cart cool stuff around the country in his massive 2008 model T908 Kenworth, custom built in Australia and the first ever of its kind in New Zealand and still one of only two here. The T908 has a whopping 15.2-litre, twin turbo Caterpillar powertrain which produces 625 horsepower.

In addition to that, like Charlie and me, he's a keen Mopar man — and has a 1970 Plymouth Barracuda 340 cubic inches. Nice! I got to spend some time in the cab of the Kenworth with Kyle as he transported the FJ Cruiser over a stretch of road out of Taumarunui. He was a bloody nice bloke.

DAY SEVEN
19 May 2011

So we awoke in Rangataua with the temperature gauge reading the big doughnut and it was still pretty close to freezing as we took off. We had to put the foot down a bit given we'd missed our destination the night before by pulling up a bit short — but I was also pretty keen to see if we could get the FJ up above the snowline.

We took some dirt roads around north of Taihape and headed up into the hills towards Ngamatea Station, which so many people, like Colin and Ruben, had recommended we travel through. At close to 80,000 acres, 20,000 of which are farmed, Ngamatea Station is the largest station in the country by stock numbers. It's a mecca for hunting and fishing with the finest free-range sika and red deer in the world, which roam the rugged splendour of the North Island high country. There's also excellent fly-fishing for trout in both the Tararua and Rangitikei rivers and some of the smaller streams on the property. We even saw plenty of pheasants!

Entering Ngamatea Station.

Big Snow was there to greet us.

The place is so bloody big that even when we arrived we were miles away from where we had to go. A couple of shepherds finally had to point us in the right direction, but told us not to run over any dogs or Big Josh would have our guts for garters. Finally, we met with Josh, the station manager, and he, Snow and Mavis looked after us with some sausage rolls for lunch and a few yarns about the station.

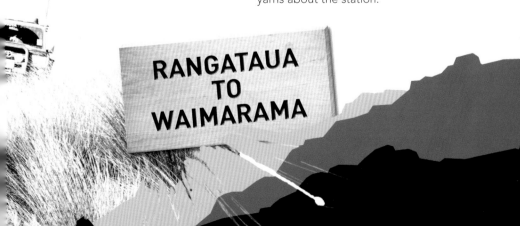

RANGATAUA
TO
WAIMARAMA

MAVIS EDGARTON

Mavis Edgarton spoilt the crew and me rotten. **She delivered us a morning tea of sausage rolls and a strong cuppa and then when we got to her place she made us a whopping great lunch of pumpkin soup as a starter and a hot ham, leg of lamb and side of beef — all of which had come from Ngamatea Station!** The meat was cooked to perfection I might add — I tried the ham, lamb and beef. And it was complemented by some freshly baked buns and a sensational salad. Just delicious. And a great feed to take our time over in the company of Mavis, Josh and the staff at Ngamatea Station, as we all told a few tales.

Mavis grew up on the Chatham Islands and watched them slowly develop. When she grew up there was no power (only generators) and flash inventions like televisions were things of myth. It was not until she caught her first flight — a seaplane into Wellington on her way to boarding school in the Wairarapa — that she saw the mainland. She worked on a big East Coast station as a cook, before heading to Australia to manage orchards. These days she loves her time at Ngamatea Station, and cooks up some amazing tucker in between painting (she's a keen artist) and hanging out with her six grandchildren in Hawke's Bay.

DAN COWPER

Dan Cowper gave us a real lesson in four-wheel-driving. Dan owns Cowper Trucks in Turakina, between Bulls and Wanganui, which churns out some of the best 4x4 racing vehicles in the world. **Dan has been competing in 4x4 trials ever since he got his driver's licence. He won his first national trial that same year and has been involved in the industry ever since.**

He's competed for New Zealand in Europe and South Africa and won a few national 4x4 trials since then and these days about a quarter of the field at the nationals are in Cowper Trucks, engineered by Dan himself. If you are in the mood for a thrill, look him up and go for a spin with him. It'll exhaust your supply of adrenaline, that's for sure.

Is a helmet and neck brace really necessary?

Yes!

That's steeper than it looks.

From there, we headed down to the gully to meet up with Dan Cowper, three times New Zealand 4x4 trials champion, and his V8 Lexus-powered machine, equipped with 80 Series Toyota Land Cruiser axles and running gear. He offered to take me for a blat, and as we were a long way from any emergency services, he handed me a helmet and a neck brace! He then quietly volunteered the advice, 'Hold on for dear life.' Bloody hell. He drove like a madwoman — up hills that seemed to be forty-five degrees plus, through streams, at pace, and at times sideways. What a thrill. While I was white-knuckled, I always had the feeling he was in perfect control. Little wonder he's the national champ!

As is quite common for Aotearoa in May, we had four seasons in one day, but as we left Dan, and headed for the Hawke's Bay, the sun decided to poke out from behind the clouds. Good job too, as we went through some of the most stunning countryside yet. The various shepherds of Ngamatea Station took us through their territories. As we approached the height of the plateau, we reached some of the most picturesque, barren, rocky hillside covered in tussock. It was just incredible. There were views across to the snow-capped upper ranges that bordered Ngamatea Station right through to Mt Ruapehu. I'd never seen anything quite like it.

How's that for a view?

I hope I remembered to put the handbrake on.

Of course all good things come to an end, and not long after this it was time to undertake the day's tarseal challenge. Day Seven's was just as unpleasant as previous challenges. One of the shepherds had a rather mischievous, troublesome working dog, which had an electric collar on it that the shepherd could zap, if and when the dog played up. My challenge was to take a few shocks at maximum voltage. A couple of bolting jolts to the mitts were bad enough but then I had to rest it bare on the tenderest part of the back of my neck. The nape, if you want to get anatomical. Holy hell! I think it left two Frankenstein bolts jutting out just under the hairline. And I'm sure I yelped louder than the dog would have. At least the crew found it amusing. It was rural humour at its rawest.

But it hadn't finished. As we left I was following the support drivers in Captain Trunky and as they went through a mud puddle they dropped the clutch and gave us such a spray they covered the whole windscreen with thick mud that even the Beast's three windscreen wipers couldn't clear. It was the first time we'd had to clean the FJ, and it was all due to a dirty, underhand trick from a co-driver!

More tracks followed and the GPS said we were nearing Hastings. Scott Lawson turned up from out of nowhere and it was pretty handy timing too because he opened up the gates, which allowed us to travel the last ten kilometres into town along the riverbed. You champion, Scott!

It looks harmless enough.

But crikey does it pack some zap!

The Beast with a bit of mud in the eye.

Riordan Kemp and Mac Atkinson at Omahu Marae.

Hawke's Bay Toyota checkpoint.

We had conquered some of the most amazing terrain, and with only minor damage to the vehicles, we were pretty proud of ourselves. There was good reason to celebrate when we hit Hawke's Bay Toyota. And boy did we get a roaring reception on arrival. Angus, the Magpies and the crew there put on a top show for all. But the car was the hero of the show, not me. I was just the monkey driving it.

A surprise gift came from Rachel Train who left us a jar of her Mrs Train's Prized Pickles. Rachel had been following the Top to Bottom Challenge on the website and had decided that we needed some of her fine pickling to keep us satisfied when we were far from somewhere to eat. They were certainly some of the finest pickled onions we'd ever tried (I hear Frank Bunce is also a fan) but the recipe is a strict secret. It was sad we never got to actually meet Rachel — surprise, surprise, we were running just a tad late to the checkpoint at Hawke's Bay Toyota, and she had to take the kids to netball. But if I'm in Patoka, in the Kaweka Range, I'll pop in and pick up a pack of her prized Patoka pickles!

From there we headed to Waimarama to catch a bit of shut-eye in preparation for another whopping day-long journey. We stayed at the Black Barn Vineyards beach house and after a few quiet sherbets and a big feed we laid our weary heads to rest and enjoyed a soothing sleep to the sound of the pounding surf.

Waimarama — means 'moonlight on the water'. How appropriate.

Luxury like this nearly caused a mutiny.

JOSH KELLEHER

Josh Kelleher had been doing what he needed at this time of the year — killing lambs. You see, for three years Josh has been undertaking the day-to-day management of the 80,000 acres of Ngamatea Station. No small task. As I'm sure you can imagine, the stock movement alone on the farm is quite a logistical challenge. It was surprising to hear there are only eleven full-time staff and a few casual workers employed for such a vast expanse.

Josh works for Ren Apatu, Managing Director of the station, and gave us some guidance from his Toyota Hilux as we passed through the beautiful landscape of the farm. He loves farming, has been doing it all his life, including two years as a shepherd at Ngamatea years back. He is a top bloke, and I hear he was quite a handy rugby footballer!

DAY EIGHT

It was a beautiful dawn at Waimarama Beach — still, calm and sunny, and the golden sandy beach was basking in the good weather.

But there was a red tinge to the sky to the south, just the direction we were heading, and as I remembered as a kid, 'Pink sky at night — shepherd's delight; pink sky in the morning — shepherd's warning.'

Waimarama Beach is several kilometres long, just south of Cape Kidnappers and, as it faces east, receives a stunning sunrise. A few long-boarders were out enjoying a nice clean beach break, and we took the FJ Cruiser and Captain Trunky for a spin along the shoreline.

Pink in the morning.

Meeting with TVNZ at Te Mata Peak.

Now there's a saying: 'If you treat a yard dog poorly it remains loyal and compliant, but if you feed it eye-fillet and put it in front of the fire, that's when complacency creeps in and the behavioural problems occur.' Sound like I'm speaking in riddles? Well, let me put it this way. It'd been a brutal few days: long hours, confined most of the time to the cabin of a four-wheel-drive moving at pace over inhospitable terrain. The crew had been faithful to the cause, but a night of comfort at a beautiful beach had corrupted a few of them and I had the feeling they were planning a mutiny and that they were going to stay put in the Bay and abandon the Top to Bottom mission.

Thank the Lord and Baby Jesus, I was mistaken, though, as soon we were headed up to the 'roof' of Hawke's Bay, Te Mata Peak, to meet Tamati and the TVNZ *Breakfast* team. All of us. Te Mata Peak looks over the Bay and at 400 metres above sea level and steeped in history and Maori myth it's the spiritual pinnacle of the region. Some of the locals from Napier prison arrived in *Thriller* costumes and Craggy Range brought some of their late-harvest wine to sample (alas I had to refrain given the day behind the wheel that lay ahead).

WAIMARAMA
TO
DANNEVIRKE

LIVING LEGENDS

STEVE BOYCE
AND MATT JACK

Steven Boyce and Matt Jack are a couple of chippies that we bumped into at Waimarama Beach. They were doing some alterations to a bach there. We had been for a burn along the beach, and they were out having smoko and spotted us as we pulled up.

Steve lives in Napier and has a 1973 Holden HQ station wagon with a 283 V8 that has a modified five-speed performance gearbox. He prefers that to the 'three on the tree' that came standard. Matt is a qualified chippy by

trade and lives in Havelock North and his passion is snowboarding.

Downright good buggers they were — and if you want to catch up with them, they're usually supping a Tui Export Quality East India Pale Ale at the Loading Ramp, the local Monteith's Craft Brew Bar, a great place to escape the winter chill in front of the roaring open fire and watch some footy on the big screen. (It's equally good in summer, actually, with the courtyard catching the sun all day long.)

GAVIN FRANKLIN

You only need to take a look at Gavin Franklin and your first impressions will be spot on. He's a character all right! **A gold-plated good bastard.** Gavin is born and bred in Waipukurau and is a digger operator in the area. He loves motorcycles and has an old BSA and a couple of Harleys.

Gavin came around the corner near Mangakuri, where we had temporarily lost traction (as Gavin himself put it). In other words, we were stuck in the mud! Hardly surprising, as that's where Gavin and his mates had been dumping all the flood damage from the recent storms, mainly mud and silt.

But all things happen for a reason and had we not got stuck we wouldn't have had a good old yak with Gav.

Not as practical as the FJ — but just as cool.

The view out the front of the Studebaker.

Sunrise over Hawke's Bay.

DOUG BIXLEY

Of all the people I have met, Doug Bixley would have to be one of the most humble. That was certainly my impression after having a chat to him at the top of Te Mata Peak early on Day Eight.

Doug had been tinkering with his 1931 Studebaker 80R All Seasons Roadster, an immaculately unmolested example of a very cool (and rare) vehicle indeed. He lives halfway up Te Mata Peak and had decided to take it for a blat early that morning and got a hell of a surprise to find a big crowd and television cameras there for Tamati's *Breakfast* report when he got to the top of the hill.

Juan, our cameraman, and I showed a bit of interest in his pride and joy, and he took great delight in proudly talking us through the performance of its 5.5-litre straight-eight engine and

the history they share together. You see Doug spotted this car and decided that one day it would be his. Thirteen years later it came on the market and his bank manager offered to lend him the money to make the purchase, such was Doug's visible fascination for and adoration of the car. He had it for another thirteen years before he fully restored it. That was eighteen years ago and he's now done over 100,000 kilometres in it.

Juan was lucky enough to get a lift down the hill in the Roadster and said it ran like a dream. Doug insisted that we all come back to the Bay and that he'd give us a tour with the top down. He's a true gentleman — and I may well just take him up on that offer!

It's a small world. Doug is a second cousin once removed of Donovan Bixley, who illustrated my *Good Fullas* book.

Two wanderers indeed.

The highlight, though, was big Barry, who laid down Day Eight's tarseal challenge, which was to sing the 'Southern Man' song in a local Hawke's Bay Tui pub … in my Speedos. And big Barry felt the need to demonstrate what he meant by in Speedos by unleashing his colossal carcass live on *Breakfast* TV. Generous to a fault, he even offered to lend me his teal-blue pair of budgie smugglers. I kindly declined his offer.

It was at that point we decided to hit the trail and headed towards Kairakau. The weather had been cruel to the region, with high winds and floods wreaking havoc. We encountered trees blown down, slips, riverbanks burst and all sorts of debris. It made for tough navigation. When we finally made it to Kairakau, we met a hodgepodge of people there, including the Two Wanderers, who live in their house bus, number-plated 2WANDA. They all warned us that the bridge at Mangakuri was washed out, but we decided to go for a butcher's hook anyway.

BARBARA AND KEVIN CLOUT

We met Barbara and Kevin Clout in Kairakau. And we were lucky to have done so. They'd just been choppered back in that morning, because there was no access in or out of Kairakau, especially for their ten-tonne house bus. Kevin and Barbara have lived in a fully self-contained motor-home, with certified gas tanks, solar panels on the roof and a porta-potty, since 2006. It's a nine-metre, seven-litre Mitsubishi Fuso with a pusher engine at the back.

Kevin had a business in Wellington and after twenty-one years of hard work he'd had a gutsful, so he sold it and decided to roam the country. Barbara was in a similar boat: having managed hotels in Thames for years, she too wanted to hit the road, see the countryside and meet new people. Kevin and Barbara got together, lived in sin in the motor-home, Two Wanderers — with personalized plate 2WANDA — and got married in March of this year, right there in Kairakau where we bumped into them.

They love getting to see beautiful parts of this country of ours and meeting heaps of interesting folk. They thoroughly enjoy the seasonal work they do too, including kiwifruit picking and packing. They are the campground custodians at Kairakau Camp, and other campgrounds, running the facility and checking campers in and out. When we saw them they'd been there for seven months, but the recent floods had played havoc, cutting power, water and sewerage there. They'd had to borrow a quad bike to get around, because the bus was not allowed on the roads until it was repaired.

There is a growing group of motor-home wanderers, according to Barbara and Kevin. Quite a lifestyle … for some.

The FJ Cruiser had been devouring anything in its path so we thought a swollen river on our way to Cape Turnagain and Northern Wairarapa would be gobbled up. But we had underestimated the power of Mother Nature. She'd really done a job on the region and we had to backtrack once we saw the state of the bridge. Even the local public concrete dunny block had been washed into the river! Ten inches of rain in a couple of days will do that. The Two Wanderers told us that thirty-three people had had to be choppered out of the area when the weather bomb struck as the roads had became impassable.

From there we had to take the long way around, via dirt roads and farmland to Mark Warren's man cave, the unofficial 'headquarters' of the Hillseekers Four Wheel Drive Club Ltd. To get there we needed to ask some road-workers for directions — one of whom was the spitting image of David Boon, the Australian short backward square. Mark is a professional four-wheel-drive instructor, and considering he was the New Zealand national champion of the V8 production modified class of 4WD in both 1986 and 1987, he knows what the hell he's doing. Mark and the team at Hillseekers have now trained over 4000 earnest four-wheel-drivers in off-road skills and how to handle mud, slopes, snow and ice, including groups involved in civil service, civil defence, civil protection and search and rescue.

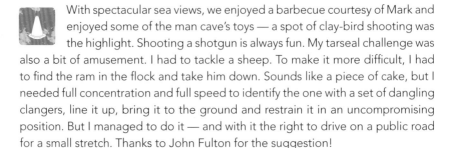

With spectacular sea views, we enjoyed a barbecue courtesy of Mark and enjoyed some of the man cave's toys — a spot of clay-bird shooting was the highlight. Shooting a shotgun is always fun. My tarseal challenge was also a bit of amusement. I had to tackle a sheep. To make it more difficult, I had to find the ram in the flock and take him down. Sounds like a piece of cake, but I needed full concentration and full speed to identify the one with a set of dangling clangers, line it up, bring it to the ground and restrain it in an uncompromising position. But I managed to do it — and with it the right to drive on a public road for a small stretch. Thanks to John Fulton for the suggestion!

The view from Mark's man cave.

Got it.

It's not how it looks.

LIVING LEGENDS

MARK WARREN

Now Mark Warren really is a legend — and not just in his own lunchbox. **Mark farms sheep and cattle on 3500 acres at Waipari Station. Part of the farm is also covered in forestry, gaining hard-earned carbon credits.** As a former national champion at V8 production-modified class of four-wheel-drive, he knows what he's doing when off-roading. So much so that he's written a book on 4WD techniques and has developed a 4WD training system. A system he instructs on his two-day off-road training course, which is basically a journey out to a campsite for a barbecue and a piss-up between two full days of hard core four-wheel-driving.

Mark had organized and prepared all sorts of shenanigans for us — but given we were strapped for time and a tad disorganized, it must be said, we couldn't do all of it. He even had a virgin track for us to conquer, one that had been bulldozed after the floods.

What Mark calls home is his personal man cave. A man cave that would be the envy of most red-blooded alpha males throughout this country. You basically have to travel about three kilometres across country to get to it. It's solar heated and solar powered — and even the rain-water supply is solar warmed. A short trip down to the beach means you can harvest bounty from the deep blue — surf-casting, paua gathering and diving for crays are the best ways to find dinner. Apparently, 'honorary blokes' are allowed after dark, or if they're really lucky, at lunchtime. You can't help but admire that retention of old-school rules.

We had some fun with Mark. Outside of enjoying his one-liners and hospitality, we did some clay-bird shooting off the verandah and helped rescue his FJ40 flatdeck, the latest in a long line of Land Cruisers he's owned. After everything he organized for us, we owe him a return visit!

Overland to the coast.

I knew the jerry cans would come in handy.

We then accessed a private beach on Mark's farm and had to refuel the FJ via a jerry can. Heading back up along a riverbed we came across Mark's FJ40 Land Cruiser, which had got bogged down in a muddy riverbed a few days prior. This called for the FJ. And it rose to the challenge. We hooked up Mark's FJ40 and hauled it out of the thick bog using the Beast's brute strength — and with the help of a snatch strap. A snatch strap multiplies your pulling power by up to five times. Before your mind starts to wander, what I'm talking about is a piece of rope-like equipment, made from stretchable webbing, common in towing bogged vehicles out of mud or sand by stretching, storing kinetic energy, then 'snatching'.

Apparently, it just ran out of petrol …

A piece of cake for the Beast.

Having done our good deed for the day and after thanking and saying goodbye to Mark Warren we headed to Porangahau and had to pull up at the longest place name in the world, which, in one version, reads: Taumata-whakatangihanga-koauau-o-Tamatea-haumai-tawhiti-ure-haea-turi-pukaka-piki-maunga-horo-nuku-pokai-whenua-ki-tana-tahu, which has 105 letters and means The hill of the flute playing by Tamatea — who was blown hither from afar, had a slit penis, grazed his knees climbing mountains, fell on the earth, and encircled the land — to his beloved. Believe this if you will. Martina Navratilova learned how to say it when she was just ten years old.

From there, we popped in especially to see Kara Scott's parents. Kara had asked that we do so via our Facebook page, and we willingly obliged.

Taumata-whakatangihanga-koauau-o-Tamatea-haumai-tawhiti-ure-haea-turi-pukaka-piki-maunga-horo-nuku-pokai-whenua-ki-tana-tahu — try reading that aloud with a mouth full of peanuts.

Using barter to trade with David Severinsen.

No faster than 100 kph, I can assure you.

Having a natter with the local
constabulary.

You're not suggesting we were
speeding, officer?

It was dark by the time we reached Tautane Station, which was our designated accommodation for the night. But a power cut had meant two things. First of all, the shearers' quarters were still in use because the shearing gang had stayed on as they had had to work into the night. And, secondly, our travelling techno-boffins were unable to upload all of the day's content onto the website.

So we decided to cash in our tarseal credit and head into Dannevirke. But the road is not a safe place as we were about to find out. Somewhere just out of Dannevirke, I noticed some flashing blue and red lights in my rear-vision mirror — one of the local fuzz had decided to pull us over. Initially, I thought it may have been because the number plate was unreadable given it was caked in mud. But it turned out he was a mate of one of the Toyota guys in the Top to Bottom crew and had only pulled us over for a chat! And he had more yarns in him than an old Romney ram so we were there, roadside, for a good twenty minutes.

As a result, we were then pretty stoked to see the bright lights of Dannevirke, a town settled and established by Scandinavians — in fact Dannevirke actually means 'Danes' Work' in Danish. Day Eight had been the longest by time in the saddle but the shortest by distance covered.

The following day would be through to the capital city.

DAY NINE
21 May 2011

So we were on our merry way to the town of my birth, Wellington, via the Wairarapa. To do this entirely off-road is a tough challenge, but thanks to some great suggestions via the Top to Bottom website and a bit of creative thinking we were equal to that challenge. We took some gravel roads and riverbanks through to Masterton.

A necessary stop was a farm we came across in Alfredton that was home to a couple of strong-minded-looking jackasses. Now, I've never ridden a donkey — but I've always had an urge to do so. And these two just looked like they needed to be ridden. The local farmer, Scott 'Salty' Kennedy, was pretty helpful, offering the useful advice of how to mount one. 'Just swing a leg over, mate.' He also provided me with a handful of hay to use as 'honey' to entice them over. All was going splendidly. I stealthily approached them then launched myself up onto the back of one who took off like a robber's dog. I managed to hold on bareback for all of about two seconds until slipping off the back. Unfortunately, though, that was all she wrote. Once bitten, twice shy, as they say, and these mules cottoned on to another jackass in the paddock — me. Suspicions ran high if I got too close, so a remount was off the cards. Time to get back into the FJ Cruiser and head south.

Off-road and, for a way, off-land.

Wairarapa hill country.

An aerial view of the road ahead.

DANNEVIRKE TO WELLINGTON

Check out those cans.

Jackasses from the Wairarapa.

Belting out the 'Southern Man' song in my tight Y-fronts.

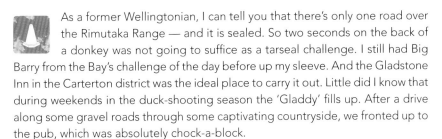 As a former Wellingtonian, I can tell you that there's only one road over the Rimutaka Range — and it is sealed. So two seconds on the back of a donkey was not going to suffice as a tarseal challenge. I still had Big Barry from the Bay's challenge of the day before up my sleeve. And the Gladstone Inn in the Carterton district was the ideal place to carry it out. Little did I know that during weekends in the duck-shooting season the 'Gladdy' fills up. After a drive along some gravel roads through some captivating countryside, we fronted up to the pub, which was absolutely chock-a-block.

There was no time to ponder what I was about to do. That would only cause unwanted anxiety and the opportunity to back down and run for the hills. So I stripped down and strode into the pub wearing nothing but my skimpy white Speedos and a sheepish smile. The unfortunate onlookers then heard me croon my way through the 'Southern Man' song. For those of you unfamiliar with the words, this little ditty champions the understated but matter of fact staunchness of the southern country bloke and talks of better beer and better broads south of Cook Strait. Just what a bunch of Wairarapa cockies wanted to hear. On completion, I ordered a quart of Speight's (bear in mind this is a DB pub), took a large gulp and headed straight back out the door. It was a real bum-clenching moment — thank you so much, Bazza!

Railway isn't road.

The humiliation meant I could travel through some tarseal to get into the Masterton railway yard. Here's where a bit of Kiwi ingenuity came into play. I dialled an old mate from Wellington who works on the railways and called in a favour. We needed to get to the capital in style. *Goodbye Pork Pie* style. So that's exactly what we did. I drove the Beast up one of the gravel loading ramps onto an empty carriage, strapped it into place and jumped in the front engine with the conductor. We then rode the iron tracks all the way into Wellington.

The crew that helped us were a funny bunch.

There was no room on the train for anyone but the Beast and me, so the rest of the crew, in Captain Trunky, took the roads in and arrived slightly before us. We had been held up behind a commuter train coming into Wellington which meant we were over an hour late to our checkpoint.

The other downer was that we hooked up a mini-camera to the train to get a few shots of the FJ Cruiser as it went through the Featherston tunnel. But when we got to Wellington it was nowhere to be seen and must have rattled loose. But our tardiness didn't appear to have deterred the punters at all. They were there in numbers.

On board the train bound for Wellington.

Just before the Rimutakas.

Held up behind a commuter train on the single track through the Rimutakas.

Arriving into Wellington.

Hoisted off the locomotive.

Pulling into Rutherford and Bond Toyota in Wellington was a neat feeling. Psychologically, we were halfway! Another big crowd had gathered, including some of Wellington's most eccentric citizens whose interest in the FJ and the journey were quite extraordinary. Lee from ZM, in the Black Thunder FJ, greeted us on arrival and I gave the good folk a run-down of our latest adventures. It was then time to socialize with the locals at the dealership and enjoy a hot dog courtesy of the Mad Butcher and a Mr Whippy double-chocolate-dipped flake ice cream topped with chopped nuts.

Dirt Box Charlie provided the ambience, belting out some cool blues-funk-inspired rock. Young Chris Gain, Hayden Lauridsen and Michael Crawford started Dirt Box Charlie as a Tuesday night jam session at the Palmerston North Salvation Army Hall a couple of years ago. Their groove and bass jazz-fusion tunes are well beyond their baby-face years and sound more like they'd be produced by musicians twice, or even three times, their age. They cranked out some well-known soul as well as a couple of their own original numbers off their self-titled debut album. A real crowd-pleaser.

Dirt Box Charlie jammed hard.

Signing some FJ posters.

The team at Rutherford and Bond got into the spirit of celebrating the sixtieth anniversary of the Toyota Land Cruiser in style that evening and shouted us a few beers once the public party was over. From there we headed straight to the Lone Star for a few more and a Lasso of Hog — an embarrassingly large portion of pork — and we recounted and reminisced over some of the stories of the last week on the road. It was a fun night and great to be back in my home town. Excitement and adrenaline were running high so we sampled some of the Wellington nightlife and it tasted pretty damn sweet.

So the FJ Cruiser had conquered the North Island. From top to bottom. And in mighty fine style at that. But that was only half the challenge and, with winter closing in fast, we still had to knock off the South Island. The following day was the start of that upcoming challenge. So with a belly full of pig, potatoes and pale ale, at shortly after midnight we got horizontal in preparation for what lay ahead.

Praying for good weather for the inter-island crossing the following day.

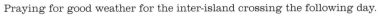

SCOTT 'SALTY' KENNEDY

Poor old Scott Kennedy was just minding his own business heading out in his Toyota Prado to work on his farm in Alfredton, **when I spotted a couple of donkeys on his property and asked him if I could ride one.** They weren't even his — they were his missus'. But Salty, as he's been called since his school days (I don't want to know why), was more than happy for me to attempt to mount a mule.

Formerly from just out of Masterton, he's been farming at Alfredton, near Eketahuna, for about twelve months. But that's not all he does. He gave up rugger a while ago, but now coaches his daughter's hockey team, the Alfredton All Stars Under 6s. It'll be interesting to see if he can still manage that when his third child arrives later in the year!

'UNCLE' RICHIE ROLLINS

Richie Rollins, or Uncle as most of his mates and colleagues call him, is a shunter, and a bloody good one at that! He happened to be doing some shunting in the Wellington railway yards when the Beast and I turned up, having caught a train through the Rimutakas. It was good that it was his shift because he pulled a train into position and handled and unloaded the Beast, treating it as if it were a newborn child.

Richie's always been a shunter, or remote operator as they call themselves these days. He's been called Uncle for years, and now that he is one of the senior statesman shunting in Wellington, his job is to keep some of the younger shunters in check. Apparently, all the shunters have nicknames like Bigboy, Biff and Bozo and a few that are not appropriate for print and best kept to the confines of the railway yard.

Uncle lives in Wainuiomata, and when not shunting loves hanging out with his eight grandchildren, two of which live with him. They're his main hobby, passion and love in life. At the weekends he chauffeurs them to sports (badminton, squash and league) while his wife does the academic and cultural stuff with them. They're lucky to have a granddad of the quality of Richie Rollins.

DAY TEN
22 May 2011

We had been surviving on precious little sleep in the North Island and it appeared we were going to get even less in the South.

Another ridiculously early start to get on the first ferry to Picton started Day Ten, via the BP station to fuel up the vehicles and make sure the jerry cans were full. But, God willing, we were going to end in Bluff about ten days later, if this FJ Cruiser was worth its salt. I was still thinking to myself that it's not every day a vehicle producer gives you a brand new car and says, 'Do as you must to get to Bluff from Cape Reinga off the road, please.' But given the lineage and pedigree of the FJ Cruiser I was pretty convinced we were going to make it.

All aboard.

WELLINGTON TO MOLESWORTH STATION (SOUTH MARLBOROUGH)

Waving goodbye to the North Island.

Our vessel.

Saying 'Hi' to the South.

The fog lifts to reveal the Mainland.

As we boarded the aptly named Arahura (in Maori meaning 'Pathway to Dawn') we could only imagine what unbeaten tracks awaited us. The weather gods had been kind — it was a cracker day, cold and crisp but calm. Ideal Cook Strait crossing weather, particularly as some of the crew had tied one on the night before — so rough seas would have been the last thing they would have felt like!

The good buggers at the Interislander not only gave the Beast and Captain Trunky the primo spots on the open back deck, they also let me have a drive of the ship! Being at the bridge of the vessel that connects the two islands really brought it home to us that this was an epic challenge from the very top to the very bottom of this fine country. The autopilot button was switched off and I was in complete control of a 150-metre-long, 14,000-tonne ship which takes over one kilometre and about five minutes to come to a standstill from full tit. Quite a different prospect to the FJ Cruiser, I must say. But the captain quite sensibly refused to tell me where the throttle was!

STEPHEN RAWLINSON AND GABRIEL FLORES

Living legends Stephen Rawlinson and Gabriel Flores actually came up to the car deck on the Interislander to give us a serving. You see we were not supposed to have been sitting in the cars up on the top deck. And Stephen and Gabriel were there to enforce that. But being good buggers they let us carry on. You see we were there uploading content on to the website and needed the satellite dish to send the images into cyberspace.

Gabriel is originally from Romania and was the first engineer on the crossing and Stephen from Wellington was the motorman. Stephen jumped over the ditch and now lives in Nelson, but that doesn't stop him being a faithful Lion Brown drinker (is it actually any different to Lion Red?). Outside of looking after the engine on the Interislander he spends his time pig hunting and deer stalking — and policing the top deck!

Coming into the Marlborough Sounds the fog horn sounded as there was some mist, which really just added to the beauty and the sense of adventure. There is something exciting about a ferry ride — it usually signals the start of an adventure, this particular one being the arrival on the Mainland in an attempt to conquer the length (and breadth and height!) of it off-road. The FJ Cruiser had survived the North Island — now it was time to test its legs in the south. The fog was lifting the further we got into the Sounds and slowly began to reveal the beautiful Mainland.

After disembarking at Picton, we headed for Blenheim. The great thing about the Marlborough region's vineyards, beside the obvious of course, is that you can actually navigate the entire region through them — off-road. And that's just what we did! On arrival at Blenheim, we were met by Craig McDermid from Blenheim Toyota, who escorted us to meet the manager of Aschworth Station, Tim Wadworth. Like all good Mainlanders, Tim welcomed us with open arms. Another typical trait is that Mainlanders are masters of understatement — and when Tim said that we were just going to pop over the spur, then over the range and drop down into Molesworth Station he exemplified that! We had to travel up and over 4000 feet above sea level for goodness' sake!

RIGHT: Southern hospitality at Aschworth Station.

BELOW: The crew lapping it up.

TIM WADWORTH

Tim Wadworth is a salt-of-the-earth cocky, who showed us through Aschworth Sation where he was born and raised. He breeds merino sheep for their fine low-micron wool, which is snapped up by the fancy Italian mills, such as Loro Piana and Successori Reda, in Biella.

Tim's a keen fly fisherman and hunter and considers the South Island just one big paddock in which to undertake said activities. He goes fishing from Fiordland to Golden Bay. He also gave us a couple of bottles of top whisky imported from Scotland. Only one of them made it intact to Bluff.

That's dinner taken care of (for the sheepdogs anyway).

The drive was both the most perilous and picturesque yet. Global warming may have its critics but that group certainly would not have included us on Day Ten. The weather was still and sunny with small cotton wool-like balls on the horizon the only clouds. It was a picture-perfect day. The views back over the rugged ranges to the Wairau Valley and Blenheim as we ascended were nothing short of breathtaking. Ridges were covered in clumps of tussock and the vastness and barrenness took us by surprise. But the road (if you could call it that — it looked and felt more like a mountain-goat track) was only just wide enough for a chunky truck like the Beast and there was a sheer drop down into nothingness. It was like the images usually sent from roads carved into the Andes in Bolivia! One mistake and it's your last on a track like this. It'd be fair to say my stomach was pretty tight and my palms fairly sweaty. Some of the crew contemplated ringing their lawyers to update their wills, but of course we were without mobile coverage which ruled that out.

After a chain of nervous moments, we had a stop to take in both the view and some deep calming breaths. We had climbed so high we could see Cook Strait and the North Island from where we were.

Tim warned that the trail got even higher and narrower. We thought he was joking. He wasn't. It got so precarious, Juan our photographer thought it safer to travel sitting on the spare wheel guard on the back of the FJ and we all had our seatbelts undone and the doors unlocked ready to jump out should the truck teeter.

Great timing, then, to take our mind off the precarious path, when we spotted a couple of wild goats — vermin around there apparently. Being men of the land, folk in those parts have ways and means of ensuring that goats, and other edible tucker, don't cause too much trouble. We had been joined by Matt Willis, founder and chief editor of *Hooked on Boars* magazine and his son Kadin. Kadin was getting ready to load up his bow and arrow to take care of dinner for us, but was beaten by Tim, who pulled out a rifle and planted a .303 bullet into one of the goats from a couple of hundred yards. We strapped it to the front and carried on — all of a sudden feeling a lot manlier.

OPPOSITE PAGE TOP: Being led by Tim Wadworth.
CENTRE: The topography didn't get any less trying.
BOTTOM: It was worth the frightening ride.

We finally get to the top.

LIVING LEGENDS

MATT AND KADIN WILLIS

Matt Willis and his son Kadin (above) followed along behind us as we went over the ranges behind Blenheim. Matt's been a forestry contractor for eighteen years and three years ago decided to start the best pig-hunting magazine on the market in New Zealand. And he did just that and has been the editor of *Hooked on Boars* ever since — a very enjoyable sideline to his main job.

When we caught up with Matt and Kadin, they'd already been pig hunting earlier that morning. **Kadin Willis is the youngest person to ever shoot a deer with a bow, as recognized by the New Zealand Bow Hunters Society, and the youngest ever Master Bow-hunter this country has ever produced.** He was just twelve when he was presented the award in 2009 (there are only eighty Master Bow-hunters in New Zealand).

Matt and Kadin were just the company we needed when we tracked through such game-rich lands.

Fording a stream.

From there we travelled for about three hours over hills and crossing fords though Waihopai Valley, better known as Spy Valley and home to the Government Communications Security Bureau and many a conspiracy theory, until we reached a 120-year-old mud-brick hunting cabin at Blairich Station, which Tim and his mates still use regularly. If only the walls of that place could talk — 120 years of shenanigans. We had a quick cuppa and soaked up the atmosphere.

The hunting cabin at Blairich Station.

LIVING LEGENDS

STEVE AND MARY SATTERTHWAITE

Steve and Mary Satterthwaite provide the best welcome in the Marlborough district. The Muller Station hospitality is world famous in the region. And they're not shy about showing it off. In fact they'll hijack you if they need to.

That's what they did to us. A couple of shepherds were sent down to block the only bridge over a river and to escort us up to the farmhouse. But I can vouch that the hospitality was second to none and we had a great little session with Steve and Mary,

and cohorts Will, Ryan and Jenna. We shot the breeze, discussing all sorts of possible business ventures and telling a few tall tales. We ended up hanging around there like poor relations but I didn't get the feeling we were overstaying our welcome. Steve and Mary seemed to love company.

Steve and Mary own Muller Station, a high-country merino sheep station with a few cattle. If you're down that way pop in and see them.

Tim tells us a few tall tales.

As it was getting dark, Tim wished us well, pointed us in the direction of Molesworth Station and took off in his Hilux. Day turned to night while we were navigating the farm tracks and dirt roads. It was pretty tricky with the lack of light, but you could feel the presence of the mountain ranges on both sides as we continued along the valley. In the headlights we managed to spot a couple of majestic stags who appeared pretty unfazed by our presence. One of the crew reckoned one of them was a sixteen-pointer.

The station we had to cross before reaching Molesworth, our destination, was Muller Station. A shepherd there, Will Wilding, had suggested via the Top to Bottom website that we stop in for a spot of sheep crutching, and initially we had every intention of doing so, but as the day had been long and the hours of daylight too short, we decided to push on through. But Will and his cohorts had other ideas. We found the only bridge over the river on the dirt road on which we were heading was blocked. By a great big Unimog truck! Will, and his mates Ryan and Jenna, insisted we head back to their digs for a sherbet or they would refuse us thoroughfare.

We had a good chinwag with the crew there, including hard cases Steve and Mary Satterthwaite, and they warned us of the handshake of Jim Ward, manager of Molesworth Station, who by now we were running horribly late to catch up with. Apparently, he gets a good squeeze on and delights going into the shake early and wrapping his sausage digits around the ends of your fingers and squeezing the life out of them. When we later did meet Jim we experienced this first hand. It's more than just a squeeze, though. He also incorporates an overhand twist and employs the straight-arm technique, meaning you're almost driven into the ground.

LIVING LEGENDS

JIM AND TRACEY WARD

Jim and Tracey Ward fed us and put us up for the night at Molesworth Station, which is managed by the Department of Conservation with Landcorp Farming Ltd taking care of the farming operations under a lease agreement. It's been managed by the Crown for over fifty years now.

Anyway, Jim and Tracey were superb hosts and looked after us brilliantly. Originally from Taihape, they've been there for ten years. They run the cattle herd, no mean feat considering it numbers over 10,000. Mind you, there are eighty horses they can choose from — all the work is done on horseback. They also run another 4000 acres over

at Hanmer finishing merino and cattle. Given the strength of Jim's handshake it's obvious he does most of the hard physical labour, while Tracey does the books. And most Saturdays they drive four hours to Christchurch to watch their two children, who are at boarding school, play sport. Then drive four hours back. Now that's commitment.

Jim was the wise-guy who used a cattle prod at full noise on me when I stuck my noggin inside the Beast while there were thirty-one dogs in it. He gave me a full-blown belt on the left buttock and I was yelping like a run-over dog myself!

Jim showed us up to the shearers' quarters where we were to doss down for the night. But it was never going to be that simple. Just as we were thinking of retiring to bed, Will and Ryan showed up again and took us out deer hunting along with all the usual accessories which accompany a hunt. As several of the vehicles convoyed through the station we spotted a few deer.

I was gifted a little reminder too of my time at Molesworth — a little souvenir the locals call the Molesworth Half Moon. You see I took aim at an ungulate in poor light and misjudged the gauge of the rifle and the bloody

The locals give us some directions.

thing had some fierce kickback. The end of the telescope caught me right above the eye just below the eyebrow and split it like a piece of fruit, or 'half-mooned' me as they call it in the area. The result was a lovely-looking banana-shaped, weeping cut. Something I'll have as a memento of Molesworth for the rest of my life.

But alas we came home empty-handed. That hurt me more than the cut to the eye. Fun was had by all, though, and it was a wicked way to end an epic day, which had started by boarding the Interislander ferry in Wellington and ended up deep in the South Island — which really is another world. We had been welcomed to the South Island with open arms by those we encountered on Day Ten.

The goat ended up as dog tucker, by the way.

We were car-jacked after dark and forced to eat and drink with the team at Muller Station.

DAY ELEVEN
23 May 2011

Putting the horse's shoes on at Molesworth.

It was a cool, crisp and frosty morning at Molesworth when we awoke. It's nestled in 'big sky' country and the day dawned as it should, revealing the beauty of the area. It was looking and feeling like it was going to be a cracker day weather-wise, as we attempted to make it through to Hanmer in North Canterbury via unsealed terrain.

Tamati and his team from TVNZ *Breakfast* had turned up to see us again and we spent some time in the Molesworth foundry casting some pritchel punches for making nail holes in horseshoes. Thanks to the heat of the embers, it was nice and toasty in there — considering it was zero degrees outside. I later had a crack at shoeing a horse. Not a natural activity for 7 a.m. given it requires you to really put your back into it. It was a stroke of luck my horse was pretty mellow and didn't mind me making a bit of a meal of shoeing him. I don't think I was cut out to be a farrier.

Four of the thirty-one dogs that took refuge inside the FJ — at the same time.

In addition to horses, Molesworth Station has forty-one working dogs. They are best friends of the stockmen and musterers that caretake the 500,000 acres, which is now also home to the biggest cattle herd in the country. Previously, Molesworth ran nearly 100,000 sheep, but rabbits had decimated the land and the government took control. Now, with careful management, rabbit control and eradication, and solely stocking cattle, soils and vegetation have gradually been restored to good shape and the beauty remains intact.

Anyway, a fulla called Justin had challenged us to see just how many canines we could fit inside the Beast — and we love challenges. So with a bit of whistling, some pointing and a few shoves we managed to get all but three of the thirty-four dogs present at the time into the FJ Cruiser. Unless my maths fails me that's thirty-one dogs. And I thought it was a squash when there were five blokes in there!

MOLESWORTH STATION
TO
HANMER SPRINGS

That seemed like a good time to leave before stranger things occurred. The hospitality at Molesworth Station had been extraordinary — typical Mainland generosity. But we needed to keep moving. We took some dirt roads and farm tracks over to the Severn River in the Awatere Valley.

It was only when we got there that Jim told us that the river was in flood and regaled us with stories of near drownings, fateful crossings, disastrous attempts and other tales of terror. Several included him as the central figure and if true it was a miracle he was standing there in front of us. He reckons he had recently tried to cross at 2 a.m., having checked the depth earlier that evening. But the river had swollen in the meantime and when he was halfway across the water was coming in through his windows and filling the cabin. He leapt through and opened the tailgate to get some flow through the vehicle and with the help of a tractor was towed slowly to safety. Even hairier was when he attempted to cross on horseback and when equidistant from both banks the horse got caught in the current, lost its footing and both horse and rider were rolling down the river bobbing like apples. Jim managed to swim to shore pretty quickly, but the poor old horse had lost all sense of balance and direction as its ears, eyes, throat and nose were filled with water. He was found washed up on a bank a couple of hundred yards down the river and needed two weeks off work to recover from the shock and bruising.

As funny as it had been seeing just how many dogs we could cram into the Beast, it really left something of an unfortunate odour. In their excitement, the mutts also blessed the FJ by leaving a couple of lovely gifts which they managed to smear over the velour as they disembarked, which added an interesting bouquet to the stench. It followed us right the way through the rest of the journey. So when we entered the Severn River, I seriously considered doing it with the doors open to express clean the upholstery, but wiser counsel prevailed. It wasn't really the depth or the speed of the river that was the greatest concern; it was more the width of the river, and the worry of getting stranded in the middle. But both the Beast and Captain Trunky are pretty good swimmers and even though the water was halfway up the door, they negotiated it with relative ease and popped out the other side to continue our journey towards Hanmer.

Powering through the Awatere Valley.

Ready …

Wet …

Go!

From there we headed down the Jollies Pass and were joined by a bloke called Graham Dally, who via Facebook had recommended we take this particular route through to Hanmer. Not long into the muddy trails of Jollies, the FJ rolled over 3000 long off-road kilometres on the tripometer. It was here that the Beast sustained the only material damage, outside of a couple of smashed fog lights, on the trip. One of the crew, who shall remain nameless, left the back door open. Now the back doors of the FJ Cruiser open with the hinges at the side so the suicide door swung open and collected a stray tree trunk as we were heading through some quite dense forest, and was crunched back beyond its natural arc. Lucky then we had Mr Fixit, from Toyota, with us to perform some surgery on the Beast and restore the door to perfect working order.

As we came through some stands of tawhai in the Hurunui district and got into Hanmer Springs we farewelled Graham, but not before he gave us a few more tips and contacts to help us get through to Christchurch the next day. We then met up with mountaineering legend Mark Inglis, who was running an army-green (or M*A*S*H*-green, as he referred to it) FJ Cruiser with black mags. Mark welcomed us to Hanmer and we looked over and admired each other's vehicles as we had a little tête-à-tête. It was timely as eleven days into the challenge and eight days left we needed a bit of motivation, inspiration and stimulation. The FJ Cruiser was holding up beautifully. The team inside it not so well. A natter with Mark Inglis and a night in Hanmer Springs were just the medicine.

Just checking we were heading the right way.

Through the forest.

Most of the fullas in the crew had a soak in the thermal springs and rumour has it a couple even had a massage. Understandable to be frank, as my sciatica was flaring up like a pack of haemorrhoids after eleven long days in the pilot's seat. We headed out for a big meal, a few vinos and then back to the hotel for a comfy night's kip.

Given the people of Christchurch had had a bit of a rough time over the past few months, collectively we thought they needed a bit of rest, relaxation, recuperation and refreshment, so we got together and organized a Hanmer Springs Pamper Pack for a lucky recipient. We asked those following the Top to Bottom website to nominate someone they felt really need a break. The winner won a night in the exclusive Heritage Hotel, and a sauna, massage and private session in a thermal pool. Added to that, to ensure they travel between Christchurch and Hanmer in style the winner would get an FJ Cruiser to use for the trip.

MARK INGLIS

Mark Inglis needs little introduction. He's a true blue Kiwi legend. **A mountaineer, winemaker, leukaemia researcher and motivational speaker.** It's been over thirty years since Mark began as a search and rescue mountaineer at Mt Cook and nearly thirty years since the fateful blizzard that left him trapped for thirteen days with the net result being such severe frostbite in his legs that he lost them from the knees down. In 2006, Mark was the first ever double amputee to reach the summit of Mt Everest.

I asked Mark if he had any more mountains to climb. Figuratively,

plenty, he reckoned, but literally — not likely given he is running out of extremities and appendages to lose, things that climbing mountains has a habit of claiming. These days he's based in Hanmer Springs, with his wife and three kids, but he's still very active. He's a goodwill ambassador for the Everest Rescue Trust and also has a sports nutrition business. He still leads treks in the Himalayas and does the motivational speaking circuit internationally.

Now I don't like the cold and I don't like heights, so I have found what Mark has done to be truly inspirational. And he's a nice bloke too!

DAY TWELVE
24 May 2011

The plan for Day Twelve was to head through a couple of privately owned farms and stations in Lewis Pass and through to Christchurch. The public had been guiding us through some of the hardest four-wheel-drive tracks and the most challenging routes, and we knew Day Twelve was going to be no different.

The first bloke we bumped into on our travels was Rick Stirling, owner of the most practical school bus I think I've ever come across. This purpose-built bus is used for doing station tours and would have been an excellent companion for the Beast and Captain Trunky over the previous few days. It's based on a Toyota Coaster bus with Land Cruiser mechanics and running gear and extra ground clearance. Rick reckons it's never let him down, ever. He was keen to swap vehicles, so we could fit the entire support crew in one vehicle (read — he fancied the FJ for himself) but there was no time for that sort of silliness because we needed to hit the trails quick-smart so we could arrive at the Christchurch checkpoint by three o'clock.

Hamish McRae met us at the gates of Lochiel Station and guided us through another beautiful chunk of God's Own along the Lewis Pass. It was a less arduous drive to that to which we had become accustomed. We took to the grass through paddocks, over rolling hills, and along some farm tracks. It was a good chance for me to take in some of the sensational sights instead of having to have full concentration on the ten metres immediately ahead of the Beast's bonnet as I had had to do since arriving in the South Island. The landscape had a certain mystique about it and there was a feeling of utter remoteness. Outside of Hamish, we didn't see another soul for a couple of hours.

HANMER SPRINGS TO CHRISTCHURCH

The crew enjoys some brief down-time in the Hurunui Tavern garden bar.

Until, that is, we got wind that a joker by the name of Ben Walker from HeliContrax was on his way over from Christchurch. He was going to offer the blokes behind the cameras a ride in the sky over Lochiel Station to catch some aerial footage of the FJ getting into its work — another example of the fine southern generosity. You can bet your bottom dollar that if this had been the North Island, particularly north of the Bombay Hills, he'd have stuck his hand out. But not Ben, a genuine southern man.

The terrain had become trickier and we were driving on loose schist. But schist happens — as they say. As we got close to the top of the range the wind was fair whipping through. And it was a cold southerly which, with luck, was to bring us some snow. It was there Ben tracked us down and we heard the chopper blades from a fair distance before he touched down to greet us. He took Dan and Juan up and followed us through the last stage of Lochiel Station — and they got some fabulous footage.

All in all we opened (and closed) fifty-two gates and forded five rivers and streams as we followed Hamish through countryside that seemed to alter between lush green and barren brown. Thirsty work it was, so a stop at the historic Hurunui Hotel was a logical next step.

LIVING LEGENDS

RICK STIRLING

We met Rick Stirling when we were driving out of Hanmer Springs. Initially, it was his monster bus that caught our attention. Rick drives a 1988 Toyota Coaster school bus that he imported from Japan in 1990 and rebuilt into an all-terrain passenger transporter. It's quite a machine, complete with a 4-litre, 12HT Toyota engine and some surprising off-road capability. It's got raised ground clearance yet it's still low enough to get under the beech trees on Molesworth and Rainbow stations where Rick takes tours with his company Trailways Safaris. He actually built three of them, cutting the floor down to get a better centre of gravity so there was no danger of rolling over, and they are all still working hard taking tours around the South Island. The other two are down in Arthur's Pass carrying people up and down and around Flock Hill Station.

Originally from Wyndham, in Southland, Rick has been based in Hanmer Springs for years. It was a love of the South Island high country that made him form Trailways Safaris, named after the original stock trails from the gold-mining days of the region. Rick has been carting tourists over these trails in his four-wheel-drive bus for over thirty years. A keen off-road driver himself, he's owned Land Rovers and recently had an old CF Bedford that he whacked a Ford four-wheel-drive engine into for fun.

Like so many of the great buggers we met on the Top to Bottom expedition, Rick was really keen to get us all back for a decent traverse through the area. He's also got a crib at Slope Point. 'She blows a bit there, the trees are leaning on funny angles and if your boat breaks down you might end up in Argentina, but it's a beaut spot!' he reckons. Rick was the bloke who told us that Slope Point was actually New Zealand's southernmost point. We took his advice on board and made sure we got the FJ Cruiser right down to the high water mark — top to bottom!

LIVING LEGENDS

BEN WALKER

Ben Walker needed some respite from his great work choppering in over fifty tonnes of goods into Christchurch for those in need. And hopefully we provided him some comical relief.

A charming chap and very generous to boot, Ben flew from Christchurch in his mate Brent Vollmer's chopper and searched for us until he found us making our way through Lochiel Station farmland. He landed the helicopter in our path and offered to take us up to get some good footage as we tracked through the amazing Canterbury countryside. It was wickedly windy that day, but Dan the cameraman and Juan the photographer ventured up for some views and fun, following us for about five kilometres.

An aircraft engineer, Ben had been flying choppers for an Emirati sheikh in the Middle East when he decided to return to New Zealand and start contract helicoptering and so started HeliContrax in Christchurch. He loves marketing and promoting New Zealand to foreigners and has the gift of the gab. On leaving us, he wished us well and warned us that our challenge would only get bigger!

HAMISH MCRAE

Hamish McRae runs the sheep and beef farm Lochiel Station and was busy putting the rams out when we needed to cross his land. He was most obliging and took us through the stunning landscape of Lochiel and through Grampians Station too. Formerly from Wanaka, he's been farming at Lochiel for about eight years. He's got a daughter and two sons, who both play rugby. That has to be applauded in this day and age when so many young New Zealand boys opt to play the round-ball sport. And dig this: he owns a Prado, a Hilux and a Land Cruiser! Legend.

The man behind me has a striking resemblance to our director, James.

The Hurunui Tavern is one of the oldest pubs in the country, having held its licence continuously since 1860, although the current building was built in 1868. When John Hastie, the original owner, was first issued a liquor licence it was conditional on 'keeping eight beds in four rooms, shelter for six horses, stockyards for cattle, providing horses for travellers to ford the river, and directions to strangers on where best to cross the river'. There are rumours, confirmed by a clairvoyant who 'spoke' with John recently, that the ghost of John Hastie, whose portrait looms from one end of the bar with a perfect view of the entire main bar, still haunts the pub. And by crikey if you were in the pub when we were enjoying a decent spread there you may well have thought this to be the dead-set truth. You see, John has an uncanny resemblance to the director of the Top to Bottom Challenge, James. James himself didn't think so and went into denial, but the rest of us were a little bit spooked to say the least.

Velma at the pub was a superb host and some of the crew were fortunate enough to enjoy a brew at the pub with our meal. Not me. I was getting pretty sick of knocking the scab off a bottle of cold beer and having to pass it on. But I needed to be back behind the wheel of the FJ to guide her safely into Christchurch. And with a bit of time pressure that's exactly what I did.

Toyota

The team at Miles Toyota.

Bylie Jean — the lucky winner of the Hanmer Springs Pamper Pack.

There was a terrific turnout at Miles Toyota in Christchurch. As usual Leigh from ZM was there to greet us and I gave an update to the crowd who had gathered on the previous few days, the incredible southern hospitality, and the amazing sights and interesting people we had caught up with. We also announced the winner of the Hanmer Springs Pamper Pack. It was Bylie Jean, whose brother, Clint, had put her name and story forward. I assured her the FJ she would be lent would be a damn sight cleaner than the Beast!

Dirt Box Charlie grooves again.

The Team at Miles Toyota put on a great show and everyone there enjoyed the Mad Butcher barbecue and ice creams thanks to Toyota Financial Services' generosity. Dirt Box Charlie were back cranking out some funk and there was a really positive vibe in the air. After all the formalities, I was a bit peckish. But being the Top to Bottom Challenge and having had to take some tarseal on the way into the Garden City, I needed to complete a tricky task to get some credits. Callum Wright, Nigel Rawson, Richard Cronin, Alary Brydone and quite a few other Kiwis had challenged me to try my hand at some car cooking. I was so ravenous at that point I'd have done anything. So I wrapped a couple of Mad Butcher snarlers in some tinfoil and carefully placed them in the manifold by the cylinder head of the FJ as we drove back to our hotel. By the time we arrived I had two piping hot bangers, which I squirted a bit of train smash on and gobbled down. They were bloody good, I tell you.

It was in Christchurch that we met up with Anthony 'Hoppy' Hopping, winner of the 'join the team' competition on the Top to Bottom website. Hoppy was going to have to put up with us for the next twenty-four hours!

Car cooking.

A finely cooked snag indeed.

DAY THIRTEEN
25 May 2011

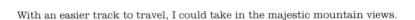

With an easier track to travel, I could take in the majestic mountain views.

On Day Thirteen we were awoken even earlier than normal, but not by the alarm clock or the daily check-in with the radio network. We were woken up at 5.32 a.m. by a 3.3-magnitude quake! It was a sharp reality check and made us appreciate just what the people of Canterbury were living through and experiencing on a regular basis.

There were five earthquakes around Christchurch that morning all at a depth of about six kilometres, the strongest of which was a 4.1 on the Richter scale at 6 a.m. just as we were getting ready to leave the hotel.

CHRISTCHURCH TO EREWHON STATION (CANTERBURY)

Heading up the Rakaia River.

It was a long, bumpy ride.

Why use the bridge when you're in a Beast?

From Christchurch we headed through Darfield for Glenfalloch Station where we met up with the manager, Chas Todhunter, and his kids and dogs. Once again the weather was superb to us. The sun came up to reveal only a few thin clouds spread across the sky like vapour trails. Glenfalloch Station is a high-country sheep and beef farm nestled in the Southern Alps at the headwaters of the Rakaia River. We were privileged to see another amazing slice of this beautiful country. I kept saying it but every day seemed even more picturesque than the last.

We hammered up the Rakaia River for a couple of hours. It was tough driving over loose shingle and through streams. Pretty exhausting stuff. What's more we seemed to be following a nasty weather front that was about fifty kilometres further up the valley from us. As luck would have it, it was moving at about the same speed as us, so while we were bathed in sunshine, the track ahead was pretty soggy. It was relief to find a dirt road when negotiating the river became tiresome. We tracked that for another hour or so between majestic snow-capped mountains.

CHAS TODHUNTER

Chas Todhunter was just doing a bit of farm work in the company of his kids and dogs when we came on through and asked if we could cross his rather large lump of dirt. **Chas was born and raised on Glenfalloch Station, which he now farms. His grandfather bought it in 1939 and the Todhunters have worked the land hard into what it is today.**

After finishing a degree in Agricultural Science at Lincoln, Chas lived in Europe for a year before returning to take over the farm. He has been slowly building up a good conference and accommodation business as well as running the farm. He even hosts heli-skiers in winter. I, for one, plan to return to Glenfalloch. It's a little slice of heaven.

He wasn't falling for my antics, and was thinking where he could best impale me.

One of the highlights was when we came around a corner to end up face to face with a Highland bull. It wasn't at all intimidated by two large Land Cruisers approaching at pace and was not in the mood to move out of our way. Like a lot of things that originate in the Scottish Highlands and are ginger in colour, Highland cattle have a savage temperament. This particular beast was no different. Hardly surprising since the breed has been farmed in some of the poorest grazing regions and toughest climatic conditions in the world.

It goes without saying that I was challenged to touch it, and of course it just happened that I was wearing a red shirt — a bull's favourite colour. It had anger in its eyes and long sharp horns that if they pierced you in the wrong place you'd end up like a strawberry popsicle! I wanted to take it for a ride, but one of the Glenfalloch Station farmers said, 'No way, mate. That thing will chew you up and spit you out.' It would have been fun. You could grab on to a scruff of his shaggy hair and ride him like a possum on a sheepdog. But it was not to be.

We were up and over some rolling hills framed on either side by the Southern Alps. I was falling back in love with the South Island. You just don't get unmolested beauty like that anywhere else on the planet; it's a slice of paradise. And on that day we were the only ones there enjoying a cool, crisp and clear winter's day.

We got to the end of Glenfalloch Station and were wished well on our way by Chas. He'd been a superb guide through some special landscape. He gave us directions and a few tips on deceptively deep creeks and other hazards we may encounter.

Shortly after Chas had said that, I attacked at pace what appeared to be a harmless slope, but it was a lot more slippery and narrow than I thought and with a stroke of luck didn't put the FJ on its roof. An inspection of our skid marks showed that we were about two inches from putting it over the bank, which would have no doubt ended the trip, been an extremely embarrassing finale to the journey and could have led to the grievous bodily harm of those occupants inside the Beast.

That is one big ginga!

The mighty Southern Alps.

Spot the trucks.

Chas Todhunter points us in the general direction of Erewhon Station.

All the while the Beast handled everything we could throw at it and more.

Sizing up the next day's challenges.

After some beautiful views of Lake Heron, we arranged to drop Hoppy off there, where a bloke in a Hilux drove him back to Christchurch. We were then back into some serious four-wheel-driving, testing the Beast to its limits on loose rock and shingle — but the FJ took to it with a smile on its face. Because we needed to get to Erewhon Station, in Mesopotamia, before dark we couldn't dilly-dally, so we had to hold on to our teeth as we went through some bone-jarring terrain.

The weather was closing in on us as we headed up the aptly named Rangitata (Maori for 'Sky with Low Clouds') River. After a tricky drive up the remote headwaters of the Rangitata we finally arrived at Erewhon. Spelt backwards, it's nowhere (well, almost) and that's what it feels like. It's the end of the road literally. Colin Drummond, the owner of Erewhon Station, a 35,000-acre property at the top of the Rangitata Gorge, began breeding draught horses over thirty years ago, and now breeds Registered Clydesdales at the horse stud. Colin and his partner Erin make sure that every mare they breed from has been broken in and used on the high-country farm for ploughing or in the wagon team. So they know exactly which ones are worth their salt and those that aren't don't have the luxury of encounters with Erewhon's stallions.

After a sneaky peak at the river we were looking to cross and the white-water rapids, we tucked into a feast of mutton, a few cleansing ales and then into bed.

The weather began to close in.

LIVING LEGENDS

ANTHONY 'HOPPY' HOPPING

Hoppy was the good bugger who, thanks to his wife, Kath, got to spend a day with us. And we couldn't have asked for better company. Hoppy actually has got a lot to thank Kath for. First of all, she is responsible for entering him in the competition by submitting the paragraph below.

Marc! I'm begging you! Please take my husband. He has an FJ40 that's as old as us! I call it a piece of shit ... he calls it honey. He has been going to do it up for years ... never does. It just drops oil everywhere and when he takes it out it wakes up the whole neighbourhood. He has been obsessing over the new FJ Cruiser since it came out. I won't ride in his FJ40 (which is probably why he won't fix it up) because it's embarrassing. I am begging you to take him so he might actually give his mistress a facelift or chuck her on the scrap heap. Many thanks, The Other Wife!

This is not the first time Hoppy's good fortune has come thanks to Kath's efforts. He could only afford the FJ40 in the first place because Kath had entered him into another draw in which he won a Vespa scooter.

Hoppy used to ride in his FJ40 when he was a kid. It belonged to the old man of a mate of his. They used to go possum hunting and carry out all manner of shenanigans in it. When Hoppy got his licence and once a year thereafter, he'd ring his mate's old man and ask if he could buy it. He finally gave up and started looking on Trade Me. When he did find one, he rang his mate's old boy for a favour — to come around and check out one he'd found for sale. **This bloke then replied that his missus had finally said he needed to get rid of the Land Cruiser so told Hoppy to come around and pick it up.** He did just that and said that as soon as he sold the Vespa he'd pay for it. And ever since, he's been the proud owner of a 1976 FJ40 with the original 4.2-litre engine in it.

Hoppy is a member of the volunteer fire brigade in Feilding and a handy small-bore shooter — at a national level nonetheless. He was watching the *Breakfast* show and commented to his mum just how awesome it'd be to spend a day with the Top to Bottom crew. Four hours after it aired Toyota New Zealand was on the blower telling him he could do exactly that courtesy of Kath's classic message. That day his face was sore from grinning and he hardly slept between then and joining the crew.

He flew and met us in Christchurch, and just quietly was bloody good company that evening as we had a few lazy beers in the Garden City. The next day he was a superb fellow crewman. It started with a hiss and a roar — Hoppy couldn't go back to sleep after the 4 a.m. earthquake. He was on a high all day seeing parts of the country he knew existed but didn't know what they looked like. A bloody good addition to the team!

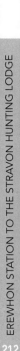

Probably the worst night's sleep on the trip — certainly the dampest.

At least we had a good supper the night before. Because we got a crap night's sleep — in fact, quite possibly the worst night's sleep I've ever had.

The foul weather had finally caught up to us. A southerly front attacked Canterbury with great ferocity. Not ideal considering we were in tents for the night. And it must be said they weren't top-quality tents manufactured to endure torrential precipitation. The inside of my tent was as wet as the outside and my sleeping bag soaked up every bit of moisture from the tent floor. It didn't get much better when I realized I'd left my gumboots outside, standing up. They'd collected at least an inch of rain.

EREWHON STATION
TO
THE STRAVON HUNTING
LODGE

Looks like a piece of cake, right?

A couple of the Clydesdales.

Erin and I prepare to cross.

Of course, the deluge meant the river was running even higher. But by no means had I given up hope of crossing the Rangitata River. Not yet … We headed up there with the biggest, fittest and strongest Clydesdales Colin could muster. We made our way to the river by farm trail and arrived to see raging white water, with that greyish tinge of glacial mountain melt. It's pretty damn high up when you're mounted on a fully grown draught horse. Mine was about 18 hands!

Colin gave me all sorts of really handy technical tips about how to manoeuvre the 900-kilogram steed, like 'give it a good kick in the guts', or 'pull its head

Erin quickly realizes we are way out of our depth — literally.

back'. My suggestion was to send someone out with a modicum of experience on horseback first. The problem was that Major, the stallion I was on, was the leader of the pack and wanted to go first. Luckily, Erin entered the river first on her bronco. It was pretty apparent after about three steps and ten seconds that there was no way in hell a Clydesdale that has 'swum' this river many times, with an experienced jockey, was going to get more than ten yards into the river, so there were two hopes of any vehicle, even the FJ, getting across — Bob Hope and no hope. It would have been one way to make Bluff — via river and sea, just not a very pleasant one.

We found an easier part to cross.

All's going well.

And then we get a puncture.

Getting directions to Stravon.

Thinking we'd dodged a bullet, we bade Colin and Christine and the team at Erewhon Station farewell and took a dirt road the long way around and back down the valley. But things went from bad to worse. Not far down the track we got a puncture. Fun changing that in the cold, rain and mud! Good job that Jared our Mr Fixit man offered to do it for us. Then we ran out of petrol. We emptied a full jerry can into the Beast, but wondered if it'd get us to civilization and a gas station. It was dark and cold, and the mist was so thick it was like rain suspended in mid air. We wondered what else this day had in store for us.

After more winding dirt tracks, fording a few more streams and slipping around in the mud, we made it to the Stravon hunting lodge, situated in the Hunter Hills, south-west of Timaru. It straddles the Motukaika River and the majority of it is covered in virgin bush and trophy animals! Red and fallow deer reign free as do Himalayan tahr and chamois. And there are also wallabies there for those that way inclined. But before we could get too excited we were told we were only at base camp, a site full of animal skeletons. We needed to head up to the lodge at 4000-plus feet.

Stravon base camp.

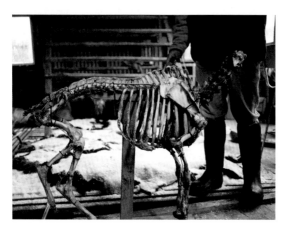

An example of the taxidermy.

A good yield.

 So after a quick squiz around at some of the taxidermatized trophies and a quick lesson in the art of preserving the skins and stuffing them to lifelike status, we began our ascent. There was one job that needed to be taken care of, however. Even though the length of tarseal on which we had travelled on Day Fourteen was as short as a sneeze, I was forced to earn some credits to pass through Geraldine. Richie and Nathan had kindly volunteered a suggestion by uploading it onto the Top to Bottom website. One that I found preposterous, but which the crew thought was worthy. I had to take a polar plunge in a stock trough. Not particularly agreeable at the best of times, but much less so at two and a half thousand feet and with the thermometer reading 2°C.

In and out in a flash.

So I peeled off the layers until I was down to nothing but my Y-fronts. And took the plunge. Complete submersion. The shock was instant.

I leapt out in a single bound and ran for the car, oblivious to the snickering and sneering of those watching with glee.

It was the hairiest ride thus far.

As we carried on upwards we really had to have our wits about us. It was some testing driving to say the very least. The moisture seemed to be coming from everywhere and visibility was sadly lacking. For the majority of the trip, to the right of us there was a precarious precipice. Had we slipped over it things would have gone black in an instant. At least that's what you'd hope anyway.

But arriving at the destination made the jeopardous journey worthwhile. It was out of this world. I felt like I'd died and gone to heaven. I was probably halfway there at least! The fog added to the magic. The Stravon hunting lodge was quite spellbinding. As the last rays of light filtered through the evening mist, we saw a waterfall carving its way down a valley between dense bush. The scenery was exactly as it had been for thousands of years.

On the menu for dinner was wild venison, and locally picked mushrooms. After another long, arduous day I didn't need a second invitation when offered a brew. Little did I realize we'd be drinking grain-distilled beverages until well into the wee hours.

Spare a thought for the Hobbits, our two content editors. Everyone finally crashed after getting a little bit sideways, but these guys need to upload the day's content. The 3G signal is lost so they have to set up the BGAN satellite. There's no electricity so they have to hook it up to the FJ's battery. It's cold and it's hosing down. The time remaining to upload reads 127 minutes. They have to be at a TVNZ cross in 140 minutes … They had a sleep of around 13 minutes that particular night.

Worth the while — Stravon's lodge and surrounds were incredible.

Even the dogs at Stravon were thirsty that evening.

At least the Hobbits got to enjoy the starry sky as they beamed away the images by satellite.

COLIN AND ERIN DRUMMOND

Colin hails from Motueka and for many years was a tit-puller on a dairy farm. But for the last nine or ten years he's been at Erewhon and he just loves it. 'It's a bloody magic place!'

Erin grew up in Fairlie and was a fairly (no pun intended) handy netballer, making the Canterbury squad. These days she's a technology teacher at Ellesmere College in Leeston.

They make a bloody good team and they showed us some fine southern hospitality! And they just love their Clydesdales. **They work them pretty hard but reckon the more you use them the better they get,** as opposed to four-wheel-drives where 'the more you use them the more they cost you!'

TODD STEWART AND BEN YOCK

I played cricket and toured South America doing so with my old mate Ben Yock, and he set us up with Todd Stewart — one of his best friends since they were five. Todd runs the Stravon hunting lodge and has done so for sixteen years. He brings international clients into some of the best wild deer hunting territory in the world.

He's adopted a few Department of Conservation principles and there's no conventional farming on the estate, meaning the habitat is reverting to nature.

Todd's always been a high-country man and decided after working in the tourism industry and taking people to the mountains he'd bring it to them. **He really showed us a good time the night he put us up at Stravon**, a night which slowly deteriorated into oblivion.

DAY FIFTEEN
27 May 2011

Once again the hours of sleep we had could have been counted on one hand, without the need for a thumb. The Hobbits managed to edit and upload all the content onto the Top to Bottom website and Facebook pages, but had had to set up a satellite on top of Captain Trunky to send the images into cyberspace. At Stravon there was no electricity or telephone coverage.

The cloud, fog, mist and rain had cleared overnight to reveal a star-studded sky. Not so clear were our heads, but we had to get a wriggle on — we were meeting Tamati and the TVNZ *Breakfast* team at Beaconsfield School at Otipua, a primary school with a roll of just under 100. And we had to make the perilous descent in pitch-black darkness.

The kids started school early on Day Fifteen.

Along the Waitaki River.

A big puddle.

We picked up two of the Beaconsfield Primary School pupils, a little earlier than the school bus usually does by about three hours. Jackson and Olivia got a ride into school in the FJ Cruiser. They were too polite to mention the pong of men, dog and dirt, but reckoned they had a blast. The Beaconsfield kids had been following the Top to Bottom Challenge since we started, and not only had some suggestions as to the route we should take from Timaru to Bluff, but also, led by seven-year-old Dougal, put together a survival pack with all the usual paraphernalia, including beer and an *FHM* mag. Mature kids, those ones!

As we headed from South Canterbury into Central Otago, the weather gods were once again bloody kind to us. We tracked down gravel tracks towards historic Waimate, before heading inland past some great views of Mt Studholme and the ranges through to Waihou Downs and Elephant Hill. We then headed up along the Waitaki River, the border between Canterbury and Otago, and the main river of the Mackenzie Basin, for about 100 kilometres past Lake Waitaki and Lake Aviemore until we came across some beekeepers near Otematata on the shores of Lake Benmore.

THE STRAVON HUNTING LODGE TO WANAKA

Ben Wai Apiaries.

Rattana Sing Sakun and her husband Jan van Hoof make natural honey at Ben Wai Apiaries. They gave us a lesson in keeping bees and the honey-making process, and even let us sample some — the smell was sensational. Generous to a fault, they gave us directions, some words of warning about the path ahead, some of their high-grade honey and a warm cheerio.

Jan was right. He had warned that the further we got into the Lindis Pass, the less maintained the passage and the rougher the ride. The ranges either side were rugged and the terrain tough. The FJ Cruiser was performing like it had just driven off the showroom floor and holding up beautifully. Unfortunately, the same couldn't be said of the Top to Bottom crew. After fifteen days on the road, fifteen evenings entertaining or being entertained and about nine hours driving already that day, we made an executive decision to pull over for some fresh air and to enjoy the silence of the isolation and to feel the warm sun on our faces. We made ourselves a cuppa from a thermos someone had sensibly packed, and just as sensibly filled with hot water early that morning. It was great while it lasted. It just didn't last. We still needed to head in the direction of Tarras and on to Wanaka.

JAN AND RATTANA
VAN HOOF

We met Jan and Rattana van Hoof somewhere up by Lake Aviemore, and they gifted us some fine vipers bugloss and clover honeys. Jan and Rattana own Ben Wai Apiaries in Otematata — a good area to have their 700-odd hives because it only receives about thirty centimetres of rain a year. We had just run out of the honey we were given in Northland so it was a timely encounter.

Not far out of Wanaka we followed a trail to the shores of the Clutha River, which drains Lake Wanaka, to see if we could follow the banks of the river to the township of Wanaka. We were still a few kilometres shy, and were soaking up the scenery when we got an absolute soaking ourselves. Of course, yours truly came off the worst. You see a bloke by the name of Lloyd Ferguson was heading downriver in his jet-boat when he recognized the Beast from the Top to Bottom coverage on the *Breakfast* show. I was down on the waterline leaning up against the FJ trying to ascertain our exact location and plotting our journey to Wanaka township. On noticing just how filthy the Beast was, Lloyd, very considerately, decided to give it a bit of a high pressure hose down, and flew past us at quite a hefty pace. And as he got to within about five yards of us, he buried the throttle and pulled his right hand down. The resulting rooster's tail showered us with about 200 gallons of ice-cold Clutha water.

In true Mainland style, he then came over and offered us some lodging to crash for the night — an offer we were quick to accept. He also let me take his V8 Toyota Lexus-powered jet-boat for a blat up the fast-flowing yet glassy river, before giving me a demonstration in stunt driving — Lloyd does nothing half-cocked, I can assure you.

TOP LEFT: Getting close to Wanaka.
BOTTOM LEFT: The FJ and I take a jet spray.
BOTTOM RIGHT: Thanks, Lloyd.

His benevolence didn't end there, though. Not long after he gave me a spray, we were airborne over Wanaka. He took us up in his helicopter to scope out some potential exit points in our quest to get to Queenstown the next day. It was surprisingly warm for Central Otago in late May, and it was a perfect day. The views from Lloyd's chopper were nothing short of breathtaking. We looked back down on the FJ Cruiser as it disappeared from sight into insignificance among the wilderness.

That evening we enjoyed Lloyd's company, together with Patrick McAteer, and we all told a few stories over a few quiet drinks …

TOP LEFT: Up for a bird's eye view.
MIDDLE LEFT: Looking back down on the FJ.
BOTTOM LEFT: The final hill into Wanaka.
TOP RIGHT: The view from Lloyd's pad.

DAY SIXTEEN
28 May 2011

After a brutal day on Day Fifteen and the accumulated fatigue of the entire trip, we decided to really enjoy ourselves on Day Sixteen. As the crow flies it was our shortest distance to travel. All we needed to do was pop over the Crown Range — easy, right?

There was a small issue that needed to be resolved first, though. I couldn't go through Cardrona without stopping in at the pub there to relive some memorable sessions from days gone by. That meant driving on tarseal. And that, in turn, meant earning credits. Our good host, Lloyd, toys not lacking, had already devised a plan. It also satisfied the many Top to Bottom followers, who had suggested experiencing the icy waters of the Southern Lakes region. The

Looks like fun ...

challenge was to wakeboard behind the FJ Cruiser in nothing but my trusty tight, white Speedos. Foolhardy.

I knew there was a reason good old Lloyd had invited us in for the night, fed us and provided us with liquid sustenance. This was it. I could see the excitement in his eyes as he pulled out the wakeboard and tied the rope to the FJ. Of course, I had to be about waist deep just so they could pull me up. It took all of about five seconds for my bones to be aching. However, he's a good man is Lloyd and he didn't leave me in the start position for too long. The power of the FJ had me up on the plane in about three seconds. For an instant I forgot the pain and enjoyed the ride. I had to have my wits about me too to avoid the jumps and other obstacles in the lake. It was all going splendidly well, and as far as tarseal challenges go, this was bloody good fun. But Lloyd was getting a bit carried away and started hurtling along. And then, as he straightened around a corner he took it a bit wide, and before I knew it I was riding the grass then doing cartwheels along the lakefront and ended up back in the drink.

WANAKA
TO
QUEENSTOWN

Looks warm ...

... but it was neither.

By this stage, I couldn't feel my hands and I'd lost all strength in my arms. I decided enough was enough. But then something odd occurred. By the time Lloyd brought the FJ back around to me, I was feeling quite warm again. And I said I'd have another crack. There was a minor problem, though. I'd lost most of the movement of my legs, which felt like they weighed a tonne each. What had actually happened was that the blood in my extremities had turned to jelly and my pump was just trying to push blood around my torso to keep my vital organs functioning. Luckily, Lloyd recognized this pretty quickly, threw me in the back of the Beast, and raced me up to the home, where I jumped in the spa pool and was handed a shot of scotch. Apparently, the exact opposite of what you should do!

After I'd thawed out, the adventure was to continue. Soon we were up in Lloyd's chopper mapping a route to Queenstown. We got views high over Lake Wanaka and the dramatic surrounding landscape. Lloyd pointed out a few tracks where we could give the FJ arseholes and then a few

That's better.

more where we might possibly just die trying to get up and over. It was quite an exhilarating ride to say the least, and I was just as eager to see the scenery at ground level.

So we thanked Lloyd for his incredible hospitality and good humour and we headed up the Crown Range overland. We were lucky to bump into Tim Burdon who let us head through his property. He trustingly handed us the keys to the farm gates, on the condition we left every gate just as we had found it. And when we asked him in which general direction we should head, he just casually replied, 'Upward.'

Heading up over to Queenstown.

The road out of Wanaka.

LIVING LEGENDS

LLOYD FERGUSON

If you want to meet a real life Crocodile Dundee then look no further than Lloyd Ferguson. Lloyd was originally a dairy farmer from the North Island, who did quite well for himself, working his way up from a shepherd, to owning a farm to investing wisely in dairying. A few years ago, he moved his family down to Wanaka and is enjoying the lifestyle to the full down there.

He's a big fan of all the activities the area offers such as shooting, heli-skiing and all number of odd adventures. In fact not long after we came through he was heading off to mountain bike his way through Africa. And he has a collection of boys' toys that would make most males green with envy. Every day is an adventure for Lloyd and there aren't many days where he doesn't do something radical. He's a big kid. But he's also a bloody interesting bloke, and what I like most about Lloyd is there's no bullshit. **He's straight up, fun, funny and generous.** Decent qualities, I'm sure you'll agree.

You can tell we were excited about getting to Queenstown.

It was a dazzling drive through some striking nature. It was a typical Central Otago autumn day — dry, cold and still. We tracked the lakeside for a while until we saw a trail heading upward and remembered Tim's advice. It was a long ascent. Soon the lake was a long way below us to the left. When we hit the top it was something special. We truly felt like we were on top of the world!

The plateau was a lovely drive across some farmland, where I managed to get the Beast airborne a few times over some natural jumps. After about another half an hour we saw a road, and having earned my penance by wakeboarding in my jocks, suffering moderate hypothermia and being within minutes of losing my fingers and toes to frostbite, I took to the road with glee!

This must be the top of the world.

The Beast with a 1928 Chrysler Six.

Personalized flat white from the Cardrona Hotel.

Not far up it, we came across the Cardrona Hotel, one of the oldest, most legendary and vibrant pubs in the country. A watering-hole that holds a special place in my heart. As Day Sixteen was the day we decided to take it easy and let our hair down, we had to stop in. We parked the Beast and Captain Trunky next to the 1928 Chrysler Six which spends its life outside the pub, and headed in.

Inside there is a collection of artefacts, trinkets and memorabilia, giving a taste of the history of the area, going back to the days of the gold rush, when hundreds of settlers came to Cardrona to make their fortunes. The Cardrona Pub is all that remains of a once-thriving town that had four hotels, four Chinese stores, three European stores and several butchers and bakers. If only its walls could talk!

Having not had a proper coffee in over two weeks, the good folk at the Cardrona Pub made me a rip-snorter and even personalized it for me with a Top to Bottom decoration in the froth. I knocked it back in one fell swoop. We then settled in for a longish (by our standards anyway as we'd mostly been eating on the run) lunch. It was a great joy to sit back, enjoy some good grub and relax. Those in the crew not operating road-going machinery enjoyed a quart or two of Speight's in the garden bar — lucky buggers.

But all good things must come to an end, and soon we were powering through Tobins Track headed for Arrowtown.

The dry tussock was gently rippling in the breeze and the autumn colours were amazing shades of orange, red, yellow and brown. The Arrow basin was far more beautiful than I remembered it. And what was even more beautiful was that we were at Arrowtown and had about an hour in our rooms in Millbrook Resort to chill before a maxi-taxi was taking us into Queenstown for dinner and drinks.

Tobins Track.

There was a really good feeling among the team that evening. An ever so slightly easier day and the knowledge that we only had three days left helped. Plus we were in the adventure capital of the world on party night! It was a Saturday, after all.

I had time for a quick meander around Millbrook, though, to soak up the beauty and the history. About 150 years ago, a couple of brothers from France, called John and Peter Butel, founded a 450-acre wheat farm to feed the miners who had rushed to the Arrowtown area in search of gold. Many of the original buildings remain, as do plenty of old grain-harvesting paraphernalia. During the First World War the natural amphitheatre of Millbrook was taken over as a tent hospital for wounded soldiers returning from the northern hemisphere. After that it was farmed again until about twenty years ago when the international resort was conceptualized and developed.

There was still half an hour before the crew headed into Queenie. So Charlie and I popped down into Arrowtown village to have a beer at the Royal Oak, only to find it'd closed fifteen years beforehand! So we knocked back a quick cold one in the New Orleans instead and headed back to meet the rest of the Top to Bottom crew.

We taxied into town and shot a few frames of pool upstairs at the Lone Star before heading downstairs for a feed. There were ten of us. We ordered ribs for twenty. And proceeded to eat them like Asterix and Obelix. It was a fun night. A bit of a reunion in many ways as we bumped into several old adrenaline-junkie mates, some by arrangement, some by chance. We let the Queenstown nightlife take us where it was flowing. A superb night was had by all!

TIM BURDON

Tim Burdon was the good bugger who gave us the keys to the gates of his farm, wished us well, told us to leave the gates as we found them (open or shut) and asked us to post the keys back from Queenstown. Brilliant!

Tim is a third generation farmer at Mt Burke Station near Wanaka. His grandfather had been farming over at Wakatipu and had noticed that the snow level was about 1000 feet higher on the lakefront side of his property. He was getting pretty tired of pulling sheep out of the snow over the long winters, so when Mt Burke Station was up for sale in 1929 he snapped it up — because it is flanked by Lake Wanaka to the west and Lake Hawea to the east, meaning both sides of the property have lake frontage. And it was a hard slog to get the property looking the way it is today by all three generations of Burdons.

When he's not gutsing it out on the farm, Tim is skiing or playing tennis and enjoying the great outdoors that Central Otago offers.

DAY SEVENTEEN
29 May 2011

Heading out of Queenstown.

I had a beautiful villa with a massive, comfortable bed at Millbrook. Shame I was only in it for about four hours. We were up well before dawn and had a huge day ahead of us before we were to get to my old stomping ground: Dunners.

We headed down Millbrook Avenue, between the oak trees that were planted in the 1860s. It was still dark but the sky was clear and the stars still perfectly visible. The Remarkables cast a bold silhouette. We passed Lake Hayes and went through the gorgeous Gibbston Valley and Kawarau Gorge just as the sun was coming up to reveal another magnificent Central Otago day. Once we had got through Cromwell we went north, sandwiched between Lake Dunstan and the Dunstan Mountains. When we got to the ghost town of Bendigo (all that remains are the walls of the bakery) we took the Thompsons Gorge Track through to Matakanui. The track winds through some stunning scenery, with views of valleys and mountains. There is quite a slope below the gorge track, which drops steeply down to Thompsons Creek, with a towering rock wall on the other side. On a day like the day we struck there are few more beautiful places on the globe. We forded a few rivers, climbed some banks and crossed some fields. It was a gorgeous day, all right. What little cloud there was around was forming the most amazingly beautiful shapes. But if we needed a reminder of where we were and the season we were in, it was stepping on iced-over puddles. Brrrrrrrrr …

That number plate must be worth some dough.

The crowd that awaited us at Ranfurly.

Every type of Land Cruiser in the country.

We were being expertly led by Paddy, a cow's skull we found in Wanaka, which we'd fixed to the front and centre of the Beast, like a Mad Max emblem. It was a scenic Sunday cruise through tranquil sparseness.

But nothing could have prepared us for the reception we received at Ranfurly. We had been alerted that there were going to be a few members of a four-wheel-drive club come to meet us and show us a few radical routes through to Dunedin. But we never thought we'd receive a standing ovation from about 200 keen Land Cruiser enthusiasts. It was truly remarkable and equally as unexpected. There were a lot of excited people, keen to show us exactly what southern four-wheel-driving is all about. There was every age group and every Land Cruiser model. Amazing.

QUEENSTOWN
TO
DUNEDIN

Of course, if the truth be known, to get to the Ranfurly Showgrounds by eleven o'clock to meet these jokers, we'd had to take a bit of sealed road through Cromwell and Wedderburn and what have you. And as (bad) luck would have it, this group knew that. They also knew they could then devise a foul tarseal challenge for me to repay the tarseal debt I owed. In fact I think they planned an eleven o'clock start just for the thrill of what they had planned.

You see, not long after they'd congratulated us for making it to Otago in one piece, they handed me a plate of interesting barbecued organs and offal. I didn't need to be a genius to work out what the little round things cut in half were. But I was at a real loss to figure out what, and from which animal, the long pizzly looking thing was. What was worse was that whatever it was, it had started to leak over the plate!

I started by taking to a mountain oyster. I tried to chew as little as possible so it would just disappear down my oesophagus without me having to think too much about having a testicle in my mouth. I then overzealously attacked the phallic-looking slab of animal tissue, but was overcome with the repulsive taste and

We got ourselves a convoy!

revolting texture and involuntarily started dry retching. It wasn't pleasant. But I had to push on. I had a couple more mouthfuls of pizzle or gizzard or whatever in hell it was and washed it down with another nut before they agreed that I'd squared the ledger. A big thanks to Jason Hancox for suggesting it on the Top to Bottom site!

So we were off to a good start! But moments after they'd forced me to eat some knackers, they began to honk in unison in a display of eagerness to get on the road, the likes I've never seen before. I faffed around trying to find my keys and get on the road. They continued to beep and blast their air-horns. I wasn't sure whether they were friendly beeps or angry ones.

Jared pulled out again.

To be honest, I was just glad to actually be moving. It was a phenomenal sight to look in my rear view mirror and see a hundred Land Cruisers kicking up dust from the dry Central Otago track. All I could do was sing the CW McCall song 'Convoy', from one of my favourite movies as a kid, *Convoy*, with Kris Kristofferson. I was the Rubber Duck!

It must have been every Land Cruiser in the district surely. We flew across the Maniototo plains, chucking up a dust storm in our wake. We headed across country through Paerau through all sorts of tricky terrain, ice, streams and steep slopes. It was a blast — until Jared, our support driver, technician, instructor and pilot of Captain Trunky, got Trunky stuck. It was just disgraceful. And highly embarrassing in front of 100 Land Cruisers! It wasn't the first time on the journey either. So we had to snatch-strap him out of there using all the FJ's might.

Move on through now, boys.

Not far down the track the roles were reversed. I went through a nasty bog, had one small moment of hesitation, and before I knew it the exhaust pipes were blowing bubbles and I had temporarily lost the ability to move either forwards or backwards. Sick of leading the convoy anyway, I stood on the bonnet and watched the 100 Land Cruisers go past. It was a pretty special moment.

We continued on for a very long time over rugged and rough topography, with the temperature not getting much above three degrees until we popped out into civilization at the back of Mosgiel. I had to take a trip around Scarfieville in North Dunedin, just to rekindle a few fond memories. But not for long, as Adrienne and the team at Cooke Howlison Toyota had put on a lovely little shindig for us there.

Every Land Cruiser in the district, surely?

Crossing a stream.

And another.

The Beast and Captain Trunky survey the lie ahead.

Fred and Steve were our guides for the day. Fred, on the left, was especially good value.

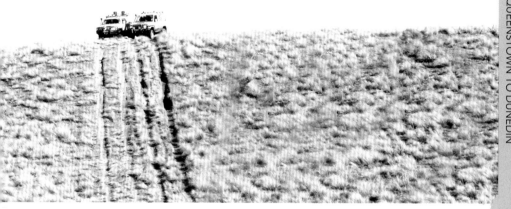

All Black Tom Donnelly's FJ40.

The turnout at Cooke Howlison Toyota in Dunedin.

That night I caught up with my old mate John Leslie and his beautiful family at the Lone Star. By coincidence we happened to dine with Jimmy Cowan, Jamie Mackintosh and several of the Highlanders, who were watching the Crusaders game. From there we looked to go out for a beer, but North Dunedin is not the lively, fun, vibrant, cultural place it used to be. The Gardens Tavern was boarded up, a sad reminder of the power of the bureaucratic fun police. The same fate had ended years of fun and life skills learning at the Bowler, all due to the myopic and archaic views of the university administration. The old Oriental had closed at 6 p.m. And the Captain Cook, our last chance, had had a twenty-first party that was all over by 9.30 p.m! So we had a jug of Triple Star Gold Medal Ale, and took advantage of the chance of an early night.

It's always hard leaving Dunners. Especially if you've only just arrived. There's always that feeling of some unfinished business. But we needed 'to take this bloody car to Invercargill, boy!'

After a good night's sleep and with the knowledge that, God willing, we only had two days to complete one of the most epic road trips in New Zealand ever, the crew was in high spirits. It was another cracker day, the penultimate of the journey, and we hit the road in search of adventure.

First up was a recommendation from Ian Lockie via the Top to Bottom website. Drive the FJ Cruiser up Baldwin Street — backwards and using only the rear vision mirrors. Now Baldwin Street is officially the steepest residential street in the world, as recognized by the Guinness Book of World Records. It is officially a thirty-eight-degree gradient. Steeper at the peak. But it was no match for the Beast which reversed up without breaking into a sweat.

The view back over St Clair and St Kilda.

The back way to Balclutha.

What could have been a lovely gentle drive to Balclutha down State Highway 1 was actually a gruelling and hazardous coastal undertaking. We did drive out quickly to catch a glimpse of a pumping St Clair surf, which was just going off. It was four to five foot and clean breaks. The early morning sun caught the mist off the breakers and it was just amazing to watch. I would love to have stayed for a coffee and a fry-up at the Hydro Café on the esplanade and soak it up. But, alas, no.

So, with a heavy heart I must concede, we left Dunedin. We took the coast from Green Island all the way to old Kaitangata, simply known as 'Kai' to the locals, a proud coal mining town, and then through some gravel roads to Balclutha where we met Ross Campbell at Campbell's Toyota. He had organized all sorts of shenanigans for us.

A little known fact is that before you can even leave Balclutha you need to pay the gatekeeper. And the unofficial mayor of Balclutha is a chap who I spent quite a bit of time with a few years back, David Latta (it doesn't matter!). So we had to pay him a visit, bearing gifts. His Excellency gave us permission to pass through his fine town in exchange for a dozen Bluff oysters. He also chucked in some words of warning about the testing topography we were to face. When we got back to the Beast and Captain Trunky, we found a sizeable swede on the bonnet. We must have been getting close to Southland!

DUNEDIN TO THE CATLINS

We cut inland through some farmland into the dazzling Catlins. It's a pretty special place, rich in history and biodiversity and with some locals that are a total law unto themselves. It was pretty wet underfoot, and we had to negotiate some sticky mud. But for me it was my chance to strike.

With only a day left until the end of the challenge I needed to get one over Jared, the pilot of Captain Trunky. You see we'd been having a running competition the whole time we'd been on the road. Well 'off' the road, in our case. The competition was to see who could most severely desecrate the other vehicle. And the timing was impeccable. We were surveying the possibility of fording a pretty deep river. Jared parked Trunky side on behind the Beast. We were positioned in soft mud. It couldn't have been better. I inched forward, slipped the Beast into rear-wheel-drive only and locked up the front wheels. I then planted my foot hard on the accelerator. The effect was better than I could have imagined. The tyres of the Beast threw up dollops of mud which went hurtling at Captain Trunky. It was a total spray. It even managed to go in through the open window and douse the dash and front seats. All I could do was yell out 'That's how you do it, bitches!' in utter jubilation. It was a moment to behold.

A grand entrance to the Catlins.

'That's how you do it, bitches!'

Morgan spits out a mouthful of mud.

We had to ford the river, and exited the other side to come face to face with a raggedy bunch of cockies and funters. True men of the Catlins heartland. They regaled us with stories of the area, and showed us around. A beaut bunch of blokes. Alan Burgess gave us a history of the Catlins, and told us a few other tales. We also popped down to see Bill Rowley's hunting hut. Not the most luxurious accommodation in the world, it'd be fair to say, but one of the coolest, perhaps. Then Gerald Burgess, a local farmer, decided it'd be a good idea to head to Owaka, over the hill.

Tyres like these are essential in the Catlins.

We had a chat to these fullas as they enjoyed some afternoon tea.

Some of the other essentials inside the cab of a Catlins Cruiser.

One of the local characters.

It's warmer on the front than on the back.

And they were off.

It appeared a good idea in theory. But there was a little downpour as we were making our way there through the paddocks. We started the climb and all was going well until it got a bit steeper and we began to lose traction. Well, bugger me! There was nothing we could do. It was like being on ice skates — we just slid down the slope. It was the one and only time I'd seen James, the unflappable director, look worried. He hurriedly put his seatbelt on and muttered, 'Oh, shit.' Fortuitously, we came to a halt before we came to any grief. Only to look up and see Captain Trunky sliding down the hill at pace towards us. By the grace of God it stopped just short of us.

Given it was the penultimate day, and we were pretty keen to get to Bluff the following day to devour a couple of dozen oysters, we took a (slightly) more gentle route around the hill. We'd also just seen the Indy 500 where the race leader had crashed on the final lap, and we swore we wouldn't do the same.

LIVING LEGENDS

ALAN BURGESS

Alan Burgess lives on a fourth-generation farm that his grandfather first bought near Tarara in the Catlins. His grandfather farmed 100 acres and when he died, Alan's father had to leave school to take over the farm, and while making a living through possums, purchased a few neighbouring properties.

But it was Alan's generation that cleared most of the Catlins, with the timber going to build parts of Dunedin, Oamaru and even Timaru. They'd clear the land, put swedes in for a year or two, then convert it to grass to raise sheep.

Keeping it in the family, Alan's two sons now run the property. Alan and his nephew Gerald were great company and took us through some tricky terrain.

As slippery as a butcher's hook.

This close to the bottom, we weren't going to risk it.

We got back on a farm track and I decided to bury my hoof. After twenty minutes or so the track began to peter out and we were in the middle of nowhere. I had Dan the cameraman with me, but there was no sign of Captain Trunky and the rest of the crew, who'd taken a left a few miles back and ended up following a dirt road into Owaka. While Dan and I calmly assessed the situation, and took a while to decide on a course of action, the others began to get a tad worried. There was no mobile coverage, and they knew Dan and I did not know what the plan was for the rest of that day. It could have been calamitous.

BILL ROWLEY

Billy Rowley was a bloody character all right. Some might call him a bit rough around the edges, but I don't have a problem with that. He couldn't wait to show us the hunting hut that he and a few of his mates had put together on a spot they thought was the perfect position. He told us a few stories of the shenanigans they get up to there — hunting, shooting, fishing for trout and eeling in the river that runs almost underneath the cabin.

After we had visited, Bill was off to cut up a pig for the fortieth-birthday bash of a guy from Owaka. He'd been shoeing horses all day. That's what he does, as well as shearing and other odd jobs around the district. He hails from Rotorua but reckons the only way he's leaving the Catlins is in a box. **His best mates are his dogs, which travel with him, not in the tray of his Hilux, but on the bonnet complete with a rug.** He'd recently buried his favourite dog out the front of the cabin. If you're in the Catlins area and keen to hear some tall tales, then track down Bill. He won't disappoint!

A beautiful Catlins Bay on dusk.

Temporarily lost.

East on the Catlins.

The crew could only wait and hope. In Owaka they found the Catlins Café and ordered a couple of cheese, tomato and ham toasted sandwiches. Step up Steve and Aileen, owners of the café, who'd been following the Top to Bottom journey online. They had the brilliant idea to check out the Beast's location on the Top to Bottom website, which was live tracking our GPS. Bingo! Steve quickly identified that we had to be somewhere deep between Lochindorb and Katea and that all roads would eventually lead to Owaka. We turned up an hour later.

That night we were staying in some cabins up in the Catlins bush so we stocked up on grub and grog at the Owaka Four Square. Being at 46 degrees south latitude, it got dark pretty early, so finding our place of rest for the night wasn't an easy task. But once there, we cooked some steaks on the barbie, boiled up the swede that an anonymous Balcluthian had donated and washed it down with some Pride of the South. Everyone was in bloody good spirits. We watched the movie *Rango*, and giggled ourselves off to sleep.

AILEEN AND STEVE CLARKE

Steve Clarke was originally from Christchurch and when his wife Aileen said she thought they should move back to Owaka, where she is from, he nearly keeled over. **But in retrospect it was the best thing they ever did and they now enjoy a lifestyle that could not be matched in many other places in the world.**

Steve and Aileen own and run the Catlins Café in Owaka. They took it on two years ago and have transformed it. It was supposed to be a semi-retirement job but they have never worked so hard! And it shows. The café is immaculately kept and the food very good. Even the coffee is first rate — they use Allpress. It's true home-made hospitality. And as they are into music it's the best venue in the region. A week or so after we came through town they were hosting Paul Ubana Jones in concert.

They reckon Owaka is like New Zealand was thirty years ago. But let's face it — that's hardly a bad thing. Their children enjoy a quality of life second to none. In Christchurch, **Steve reckons you didn't know the people two doors down from you, but in the Owaka district you know every one of the 400 residents.** They certainly know Steve and Aileen and are grateful they have brought some atmosphere to the Catlins Café.

DAY NINETEEN
31 May 2011

After a cosy night's sleep in the cabins, we were awoken by the radio network at 5.30 a.m. enquiring as to our whereabouts and keen on a run-down of the previous day's progress and antics.

From there we leapt into the Beast and headed down to Curio Bay to catch up with Tamati for the last time. When we got there it was still dark, but an astounding number of locals and tourists had turned up. Quite staggering considering the total population of Curio Bay only peaks at about eighteen people.

268

TOP LEFT: A surprisingly big crowd at Curio Bay.

TOP RIGHT: The campground at dawn.

BOTTOM LEFT: The last live cross with TVNZ.

BOTTOM RIGHT: Lining up for pies and muffins.

The Beast getting plenty of attention.

Curio Bay is an absolute national treasure, one of the finest examples of a Jurassic fossilized forest in the entire world. After the sun came up — pretty late it must be said, but worth the wait as we saw it rise over the headland on the horizon — we saw beautiful Porpoise Bay in all its glory. A sweeping golden sand beach, home to seals, sea lions, yellow-eyed penguins and even pods of rare Hector's dolphins. But it is the 170-million-year-old fossils that hold the most interest. Petrified stumps, fallen trees and fern imprints are in full view, all as a result of a process called silicification that took place when New Zealand was still linked to the ancient Gondwana supercontinent.

The campground where we met was nestled in among flax and tussock. The sun seemed to take forever to come up, which wasn't ideal as Tamati kept coming out with gaffes on live TV about what prizes were up for grabs, how many kilometres we'd done and a few other beauties. But when it did come up over the peninsula it was stunning. The waves were rolling in and the beach was golden and empty.

Famous in the Catlins are the Possum Pickers — a group of hillbilly musicians. As I was walking over through the car park I saw a lady with a banjo. I said that I thought it was a joke about everyone from the Catlins being banjo players and she replied, 'Good one, man. Give me a high six!' I must admit to checking for the sixth digit before slapping hands with her.

THE CATLINS TO BLUFF

Daybreak on the last day.

The Possum Pickers pumped out a couple of ditties that went down well. It added to the atmosphere. We were all pretty fired up; it was the last day, after all!

Before we could hit the tracks I popped in to pick up a steak and cheese pie for breakfast from Val and Steve at the Curio Bay Holiday Park store. In typical Southland style, one of the local ladies, June Stratford, had baked a bunch of muffins, so I finished with one of those and strong coffee from the machine. All that awaited was four hours off-road and we'd be at the goal — the bottom, all the way from the top!

And we were off through some farmland to Slope Point, the southernmost tip of the South Island. Bluff may be the spiritual southernmost point of mainland New Zealand, but Slope Point lies at 46°40'31.39"S, 169°0'20.34"E, being the southern tip of the South Island.

Good old Barry Brown, the joker who manages the southernmost farm in the South Island and whose permission you must seek to cross said farm to reach the coastline at Slope Point, was a good bugger and escorted us down there on his quad bike. The weather was wet, cold and a bit miserable, but 'Brownie' thought it was quite a reasonable day.

After a couple of photo opportunities for me and the crew, we were back around the coast to Fortrose via tracks, and from there through some farmland towards Bluff. We arrived at a crossroads and as we all piled out of the cars while we decided where we needed to go, the excitement and emotion of knowing we were within spitting distance of our final destination was evident. Someone pulled out a hacky sack and we played that for probably half an hour in between recounting stories, giving each other gyp and laughing away.

VAL WHYTE AND STEVE HILL

271

Steve Hill and Val Whyte have been running the Holiday Park at Curio Bay for five years. Steve is from Christchurch and he met Val, who's from Southland, in Queenstown. **Absolute salt-of-the-earth folk.** So much so that when we broadcast the TVNZ *Breakfast* show from their campground at sparrow's fart on Day Nineteen, local legend June Stratford baked some blueberry muffins out of the blue to give them a hand.

They keep an eye on the wildlife in the area such as the yellow-eyed penguins, seals, Hector's dolphins and sea lions. Not long before we arrived, Steve had gone over to restock and clean up the ablutions area and left the store open. **When he came back a massive adult sea lion was wandering around the store — inside! There was no way he could entice him out, so Steve had to climb in the back window and chase him out with a broom!** Not before the sea lion had ripped the cord to the phone and the coffee machine out.

When not working, Steve and Val enjoy collecting the bounties of the Pacific Ocean off the Catlins coast. Their catch is mainly blue cod, trumpeters and the odd groper, and in summer includes crays and school sharks. If only the Catlins were a few degrees warmer …

Brownie leads the way.

The southernmost point of mainland New Zealand.

Local farmers Rob and his dad Matt Mainland saw us from the paddocks and came over for a chat. It was when Matt told us that we were still some way from Bluff, and that the farm tracks were pretty slippery, that we decided we'd better get cracking. We had a date with the Mayor, the Honourable Timothy Shadbolt, at twelve o'clock sharp. That was one hour away and Matt had said we had an hour and a half's drive.

We shot the gap immediately, but as fortune would have it we struck a Southland traffic jam. We got stuck behind a hundred or so cattle being mustered into another paddock and had to follow them as they meandered down the track at a snail's pace, dropping their guts as they went. There's something special about the smell of cowshit and mud on a hot radiator. And that was what we had most of the day. But for now we were in a hurry.

Slope Point.

The crew are pretty stoked.

The crew are feeling festive and break into a hack.

LIVING LEGENDS

BARRY 'BROWNIE' BROWN

Good old Barry Brown was waiting, unbeknown to us, at the gates of the 1000 acres he manages, which is the only access to Slope Point, mainland New Zealand's southernmost point. And a bloody good job he was or we would have to have forfeited going here or done it illegally!

But it was a blessing Brownie was there because he was a true blue cocky and a gold-plated good bastard. He's originally from Fortrose, which is about twenty kilometres down the road, has

been a shearer for about thirty years and has been farming for ten.

You've got to admire him. He played club rugby until he was fifty-five! In the bloody forwards at that. For over thirty-five years, you'd see him sipping DB Draught down at the Tokanui footy club on a Saturday after another bruising encounter. In the last few years he's moved into bowls but laments the cost to play such a soft sport. Get your boots back on, reckon, Brownie!

ROB AND MATT MAINLAND

We bumped into Rob and his dad, Matt Mainland, when we got a bit lost in the Deep South, not far from our final destination, Bluff. We had pulled over, turned the stereo up, and begun to play hacky sack when they came over and gave us a few directions on how to get through to Bluff without using tarseal. Rob and Matt have a 500-acre sheep farm and were heading out to muster when they came across our motley crew.

Matt grew up in nearby Mabel Bush, and has been on his present farm for twenty-eight years. Rob grew up there and played footy at the mighty Woodlands Rugby Football Club where (interestingly) he'd drink both Speight's and Tui and feel a loyalty to both drops.

They're both bloody good shearers and Matt sheared 300 sheep in a day at the age of sixty!

275

The 'Bolt' was at Land's End bearing Bluffies. Thanks, Tim.

The crew celebrate.

Disaster was averted when the farmer caught sight of us and let us past. From there we motored through to Bluff, where Tim the Bolt was waiting for us in his full mayoral get-up, complete with pirate's hat, fur-lined cape, medals and mayoral gown. And what was best was that he had two dozen fresh Bluff oysters which, after I shook his hand, he offered me and I gladly accepted.

We'd been talking about the oysters for nineteen long days and it was pretty bloody emotional to finally be at Land's End where State Highway 1 finishes, looking out towards Stewart Island and having a salty Bluff oyster slipping down my throat.

It was special to say the least. We could only think back and ponder. All the support we got from the wider Top to Bottom team. And particularly from the public who took us in, fed us, gave us decent directions, gave us dud directions, kept us company, and made the journey one of the most amazing times of our lives.

TIM SHADBOLT

His voice is unmistakable, his laugh is contagious. He's the former mayor of Waitemata and the current mayor of Inver-Vegas. He's Tim Shadbolt (pictured with Neeraj from Toyota).

I've always been a fan of the Bolt, but I never realized just how happy I'd be when I saw him at Land's End in Bluff after travelling 5000 gruelling kilometres.

He was there with a smile as wide as the horizon, in his full regalia and had two dozen chilled Bluffies in his hand.

It was quite a way to end what had been a journey of epic proportions and Tim was just the man to end it with a bit of pomp and ceremony and a few of his giggles.

A pensive moment reflecting on what we had achieved.

There was silence in both vehicles as we drove back to Invercargill from Bluff. It slowly began to sink in that the epic adventure was over. We reflected on all the beautiful country we had seen and the amazing people we had met and felt proud to be New Zealanders.

Back in Invercargill, we had a marvellous knees-up at GWD Toyota. Celebration was in the air, there were more of the finest Bluff oysters being served on ice with fresh lemon juice and cracked black pepper and our old mates Dirt Box Charlie were belting out some numbers.

But it was Toyota Ambassador Dave Dobbyn who stole the show and with his silky voice raised the roof with some of his classics like 'Slice of Heaven', 'Whaling' and 'Loyal' and other songs from the soundtracks of most Kiwis' lives. When he started strumming 'Welcome Home' it pulled heavily on the heartstrings and a few of the team got a bit teary-eyed. We'd been through a hell of a lot over the nineteen days of the trip.

We had a question and answer with the team at GWD Toyota and some of their clients. Given it was the last day, I gave a few fairly frank answers and praised those in the Deep South for being a lot more generous than those in the Shallow North. (I was promptly offered another couple of oysters and a blisteringly cold beer.) When Dave Dobbyn asked me, 'How were the testicles?' I thought he said 'How are the testicles?' Such a forthright question deserved an equally direct answer, so I replied, 'To be honest, Dave, after nineteen days on the road and a couple of dozen oysters, they're about to explode!' He, of course, was referring to the sheep's cods I had eaten back in Ranfurly.

DAVE DOBBYN

Another Kiwi for whom little intro-duction is needed is Dave 'DD' Dobbyn. Most New Zealanders know by heart at least half a dozen of the songs he's written. And a few of those he cranked out at the GWD Toyota dealership in Invergiggle at the conclusion of the Top to Bottom Challenge on Day Nineteen.

Dave's dazzling music career started with his mates from Sacred Heart College when they formed the rock band Th' Dudes and produced such epic numbers as 'Be Mine Tonight' and 'Bliss'. After Th' Dudes he formed post-punk group DD Smash ('Outlook for Thursday' and 'Whaling'). Since then

he's had an amazing solo career and quite rightly became an officer of the New Zealand Order of Merit in 2002.

His voice was as silky and smooth as ever that afternoon in Invercargill and he had the punters there spell-bound. Just Dave and his guitar. Not only that, he chatted away to all and sundry as happy as Larry when he wasn't strumming the six string too. He stuck around with us for a while after he'd finished his second set, then had to rush off and catch a flight to celebrate his wife's birthday back in Auckland. One of New Zealand's genuine legends and just a lovely, lovely down-to-earth fulla, indeed.

The entire team at GWD Toyota.

Restored FJ40 winner as proud as punch — and why wouldn't you be?

It was with Bob and the team at GWD Toyota that we announced the winner of the fully restored, from the ground up, 1978 FJ40. I rang Dylan and he couldn't believe his luck. I'm positive the other 9000 people following Top to Bottom on Facebook couldn't either!

That night in Invergiggle, the Lone Star once again turned it on for us. The mood was one of delight, accomplishment, relief, sadness, exhaustion, exhilaration, and all the other emotions related to the end of an epic journey. The adventure had been taxing but hugely rewarding, and I don't mind saying we were pretty proud of ourselves. And we celebrated in a fitting manner.

The next morning I flew out early and while I couldn't wait to see family and get back into a bit of a routine (and get a good night's sleep), there was an empty feeling. With no adventure and camaraderie to get the adrenaline flowing that day, I got a fraction melancholic, missing the good bastards I had met and got to know on the tour. We had been on a road trip like no other before it. It was tough at times, a gruelling schedule and high intensity for fifteen to eighteen hours a day for nineteen days. But it will never ever be forgotten by the thousands of people up and down the country who came in contact with it.

It was an extraordinary means of celebrating sixty years of Toyota Land Cruiser and introducing the latest in a long line of models to New Zealand. It had been done!

THE BIOGRAPHY OF A LEGEND

Vehicle Heritage

Land Cruiser
Model BJ Series
Production Period 1951-1955

*Production period in Japan.
The period of introduction for this generation model may vary by region.

The BJ

In 1951 the Toyota Motor Corporation developed a prototype of the BJ, a military light utility vehicle, which came about due to the demand for this type of vehicle in the region at the time. It ran a 3.4-litre, six-cylinder petrol engine which generated 85 horsepower and came with two front seats and a rear bench which could fit another two, or three at a real crush. Back then it was unimaginable to match a compact chassis with a truck engine. And, as a result, one of the Toyota engineers, Ichiro Taira, who designed the BJ and was apparently a top bloke, had a mountain to climb, both figuratively and literally, to convince Toyota's senior management just how cool the BJ was. So he took it for a test drive and didn't stop until he had got halfway up Mt Fuji — higher than any vehicle had ever gone. A legend was born! The result was just what the market was yearning for.

The Japanese National Police heard about this feat, were pretty darn impressed and promptly ordered 289 with plans to officially adopt it as their lead patrol car. It was originally only built for specific orders like this, including one from the Yanks who needed 100 over in Korea at the time.

Land Cruiser
Model 20 - 30 Series
Production Period 1955-1960

*Production period in Japan.
The period of introduction for this generation model may vary by region.

The 20–30 Series

In 1954 the BJ had started to become popular and was in hot demand so it was renamed the Land Cruiser and mass production began. Its engine got an upgrade to a 3.8-litre, 125-horsepower doozy. It went through a few minor transformations — in 1955 it got a facelift and some more stylish bodywork so that it had more civilian appeal, particularly for export markets. Later it became a smoother ride thanks to longer four-plate leaf springs which were being used on Toyota's light truck. In 1957 the Land Cruiser was sold as far away as Brazil and Australia and was chosen as the vehicle to spearhead Toyota's drive into export markets outside of Japan. Toyota's growth strategy was to avoid entering markets that had existing automobile industries so they targeted South and Central America, South-East Asia and the Middle East. What's more, these markets required vehicles that could handle some pretty bloody tough driving conditions and terrain, and the Land Cruiser lapped up that sort of stuff like a pussycat does milk.

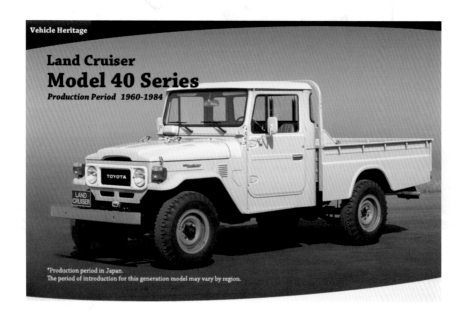

The FJ

It was in 1960 that the now iconic FJ40 Series was launched. Mechanically, the FJ40 was powered by a 3.9-litre, 125-horsepower engine and came with low-range gearing for the first time as well as synchromesh on the third and fourth gears. It was available in hard-top, soft-top and pick-up versions, all with a short wheelbase. The 90-inch wheelbase sure was short, but it was excellent for climbing up and over bumpy and rocky terrain. It was a hefty 3470 pounds — just to put it into perspective the Corolla of the sixties was less than half that at 1560 pounds!

By 1965 the FJ40 was the best-selling Toyota in the United States, and by 1968, the 100,000th Land Cruiser was sold worldwide. But that was just the start of an exponential explosion. In 1972, the 200,000th was sold, and blow me down in 1973 the 300,000th and on it went. In 1969 it arrived in New Zealand courtesy of the Toyota plant that existed in Christchurch — available in short wheelbase with a raised roof for improved visibility (made of resinous materials instead of steel panelling so as not to be top heavy) and long wheelbase, a favourite workmate of Kiwi farmers and contractors.

Various improvements to the mechanics, performance, handling and accessories were carried out for the healthy lifespan of twenty-four years that Toyota produced the FJ40 until the model was finally shelved in 1984. Diesel engines, front disc brakes, two-speed electric wipers, padded steering wheels and dash, front towing hooks, four-speed fully synchronized transmissions, emergency lights with extension cords, floor carpets, electric winches and heaters and defrosters were all crowd favourites with the punters. The switch from two-wheel-drive to four-wheel-drive was made by engaging or disengaging the front-wheel-drive with the use of an engine-vacuum actuator.

Today the FJ40 has become a real enthusiast's vehicle and is coveted by collectors all over the world, including right here in God's Own Country. Although it'd be only fair to add that many of those FJ40s still alive are not sitting in museums or only driven on summer Sundays. They are often used as workhorses in some of the toughest situations, as I witnessed on the Top to Bottom escapade.

The model commanded such a loyal following because it had many a unique feature that intrigued motor and four-wheel-drive enthusiasts. As a silly little example, it had a removable roof and doors, and you could even take the windscreen off, bringing a new meaning to the term 'convertible'. Grease monkeys and bogans loved them too, because of their compatibility with General Motors small-block engines, which could be dropped into them with little drama and hooked up to the Toyota gearboxes with ease. It was hugely revered for its rugged robustness, reliability and practicality and testament to that are the many still in action today. In fact you can still buy FJ40 parts at most Toyota parts and service departments.

The 55 Series

Another one of my favourites — possibly the ugliest yet coolest-looking vehicle — and clearly the design that most Remuera Tractors try to emulate to this day. It looked a bit like an oversized Volvo station wagon with knobby tyres. The 55 Series was produced between 1967 and 1980, and had different monikers around the world including the Moose and the Iron Pig. It was really popular here and a favourite in the Aussie outback where the folk need utter reliability, given they can't afford to have their vehicle crouch in remote parts far from water and others.

The 1975 Land Cruisers with some cool-looking cats operating them.

Vehicle Heritage

Land Cruiser
Model 60 Series
Production Period 1980-1989

*Production period in Japan.
The period of introduction for this generation model may vary by region.

The 60 Series

Built from 1980 to 1989, the 60 Series was designed with a more luxurious interior and a more comfortable ride and changed the way the world thought about four-wheel-drive vehicles. The luxury GX model came with the choice of a four-litre diesel engine, a high roof body, a five-speed transmission, and other cool features like remote-control mirrors and (my favourite) an electric moon roof. The engine was the first diesel offered in the Land Cruiser Series. And the 60 Series was also upgraded to electric fuel injection, resulting in more power and better fuel consumption.

The 60 Series was made in the eighties so the colours needed to be flamboyant. The range included Cognac, Rootbeer, Freeborn Red, Stardust Silver and Desert Beige. In 1991 the one millionth Toyota Land Cruiser was sold.

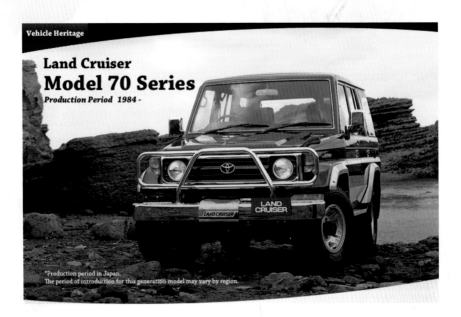

Vehicle Heritage

Land Cruiser
Model 70 Series
Production Period 1984 -

LAND CRUISER

*Production period in Japan.
The period of introduction for this generation model may vary by region.

The 70 Series

In 1984, even though the 40 Series was still hugely popular after thirty years, time had come for a total redesign. There was no way in the world Toyota were going to compromise on the inherent brutal toughness, however. Body plates were actually thickened and other features added. An automatic transmission was introduced, making the 70 Series Land Cruiser the first Japanese four-wheel-drive vehicle available in automatic. In 1996 two 70 Series Land Cruisers were first and second in the gruelling Paris to Dakar race.

The 70 Series is still in production today — and Captain Trunky, the support vehicle on the Top to Bottom Challenge, is a fine example of this specimen.

The Prado

In 1990 the 70 Series underwent a total makeover and the result was named the Prado, which also is still in production today. The four-door model back then had three rows of seats and could lug eight people around, comfortably. The Prado got wide body versions in 1991, my first year in Dunedin, and in 1996 the Prado became a stand-alone model in the Toyota stable.

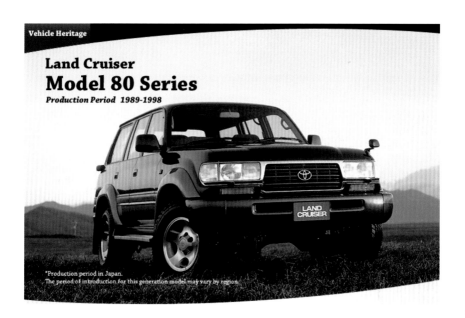

Land Cruiser
Model 80 Series
Production Period 1989-1998

*Production period in Japan.
The period of introduction for this generation model may vary by region.

The 80 Series

The 80 Series came along in 1990 attempting to fill the big shoes of the 60 Series, which by the late eighties had become more of a family vehicle and town car for city slickers than an all-terrain vehicle. So the 80 Series was designed with leading-edge technology and comfort features. At five metres long and two metres wide it had the most commanding presence on the road, and if you were in the market for one, you could choose between three different grunty engines. In 1996 all models adopted airbags and ABS brakes as standard issue and the dashboard was modelled on a grand piano. Leaf springs were replaced with coil springs in the front and rear suspension and the arms supporting the axle had rubber bushings on the pivot portion, which reduced vibrations and shocks coming from rough rides.

Tough, but with plush comfort and a smooth ride, the Land Cruiser 80 Series, built until 1997, was true to enduring Land Cruiser values and it could still get you through, up and over the roughest roads and toughest trails going. Its wide tyres and large fenders gave it a bold chunky look, some comparing it to a luxury battleship cruising the streets.

*Production period in Japan.
The period of introduction for this generation model may vary by region.

The 90 Series

The 90 Series Prado incorporated the first independent suspension ever put on a Land Cruiser, with the upper arm mounted in a higher position to strengthen the overall resistance of the suspension to horizontal G force. It also came with faux wood panelling on the instrument panel, which is always nice.

But I can sum it up pretty damn quickly. Built from 1996 to 1998 it was wide and low and, in my opinion, superior in every aspect to the Mitsubishi Pajero (and we all know what Pajero means in Spanish).

Land Cruiser
Model 100 Series
Production Period 1998-

*Production period in Japan.
The period of introduction for this generation model may vary by region.*

The 100 Series

The Toyota Land Cruiser 100 Series had a pretty rigorous reputation to protect when it was introduced in 1998. The 80 Series, which it replaced, was widely respected and regarded for its high performance on crap roads, its manoeuvrability and invariable reliability — which made it the clear vehicle of choice for the United Nations and NATO and the tricky situations and locations those organizations find themselves in. For even further improved performance, two new leading-edge power units, mechanically engineered for low fuel consumptions and resulting low emissions — to satisfy both the penny-conscious, given rising gas prices, and the global warming believers. Having said that, one of them was a meaty V8 with a piston displacement of 4663 cubic centimetres and 32 valves. This was the first ever V8 in a Toyota-branded car. The front suspension was upgraded to a double wishbone, independent version with rack and pinion steering. The 100 Series had become the pinnacle of off-road vehicles. Total global production of Toyota Land Cruisers by 2000 was 3,720,000 — the same as the population of New Zealand at the time!

Vehicle Heritage

Land Cruiser
Model 120 Series
Production Period 2002-

*Production period in Japan.
The period of introduction for this generation model may vary by region

The 120 Series

The 120 Series was a full-monty four-wheel-drive but when behind the wheel the driver endured less road, wind and engine noise than most luxury sedans. What's best is that it came with DAC and LSD. That stands for Downhill Assist Control, which helps with stability when tackling some steep downward slopes, and Limited Slip Differential, which allows for some difference in angular velocity of the output shafts. In addition to DAC, it was equipped with HAC (Hill-start Assist Control) which kicked in when going back up the slope. The 120 Series was manufactured from 2002 to 2009.

The 200 Series

The 200 Series offers numerous extra features and upgrades such as a lighter but stronger frame and the option of a V8 diesel. These days the Land Cruiser is still the king of four-wheel-drive beasts by a rural mile. And it eats up the road like no other too. Basically, if you are the proud owner of a Land Cruiser you can take on any track, any time, knowing you are supported by state-of-the-art off-road technology. The 200 Series is the latest Land Cruiser, one of the longest continued model cycles in the Toyota line-up.

The FJ Cruiser

The FJ Cruiser is a true-blue tribute to the FJ40, first introduced in 1960. The heritage is clear with its bold retro styling, including the white roof, familiar front nose and flared guards. It is the only current Toyota to have the name TOYOTA written across the front grille instead of the corporate emblem (the one that looks like a bean wearing a sombrero). But its technology is anything but retro! After four million Land Cruisers manufactured, Toyota knows a thing or two about what works and what doesn't. It comes complete with automatic disconnecting front differential and rear differential lock, a four-litre powertrain with a five-speed automatic gearbox. Vehicle Stability Control (VSC) adjusts engine power and braking to help the vehicle maintain the direction in which it is being steered. You can also switch to two-wheel-drive for better fuel consumption and economy. Safety is fully taken care of with ABS brakes, enhanced with electronic brake force distribution and eight airbags. And there is nothing retro about the accessories either. The steering wheel has audio and bluetooth controls, and there's auxiliary and USB inputs to crank out your MP3 player. And dig this — a reversing camera integrated into the rear vision mirror. Its windscreen is almost vertical and comes with three wipers for maximum surface clearage.

Interestingly, the FJ Cruiser was not initially intended for sale but due to the enormous response the prototype got at the North American International Car Show it went into production. And I was lucky enough to test drive one in some of the most beautiful and remote parts of the planet!

INTRODUCING
THE TOP TO BOTTOM CREW

We were bloody fortunate that we had the crew we did. Had there been a weak link, a moody bugger or an arsehole, the trip would have been extremely unpleasant (above and beyond the unpleasant aromatic atmosphere of nine or ten blokes in two cars). This group became really tight and gelled instantly with the positive energy enduring all the way to Bluff. It was a privilege to be in their company.

The following was written by the crew, about the crew.

Marc Ellis

MACCAROON

The crew thinks Marc relates incredibly well to almost every living person and is liked anywhere he goes. His performances, stories and competitiveness kept the crew entertained for the entire three weeks. From setting a challenge as to who could eat the most Lone Star ribs, to impersonating an Indian taxi driver on the CB radio, his high jinks and energy were infectious and his focus remarkable. His ability to get straight up and function fully after a few hours' sleep and be signing Top to Bottom posters with a smile on his face twelve gruelling hours later was truly remarkable. Marc never takes anything on half-cocked.

We'd all like to thank him for making this trip the most amazing time of our lives.

James McDonald
JIMMY McD

James had the toughest role on the trip by far — Camp Mother. He had to manage Marc, which is a full-time job in itself. He also had to manage the production crew during the day and night, field the call from the radio network and TVNZ at sparrow's fart, deal with Toyota Head Office, plan the

itinerary and organize and access the route with landowners for the next day and accommodation further down the line. He was also the timekeeper, making sure we got to the dealer checkpoints and TVNZ crosses on time. There literally weren't enough hours in the day for him. If he didn't want to speak to it, film it, or edit it, then it didn't need doing. On top of all that he managed to get nine guys and all their gear into the trucks every morning while the rest of us were coming to our senses — without uttering so much as an angry word. But he still managed to find the time to unwind with a few brews in the evening and head out geese shooting now and then. Plus he had the dubious honour of winning the beard-growing competition — hands down.

Juan Mon
JUANITO

Juan is a naturally gifted photographer with a massive bag of tricks. It was incredible just how quickly he could sum up a location and pick the best angle for the shot. A typical example was when we arrived at the river just out of Wanaka, and when he saw a jet-boat heading for us at pace was up a willow

tree like a rat up a drainpipe. The resulting shot was a masterpiece. Unfortunately, poor old Juan suffers terribly from carsickness, not great when you are sitting in the back of a car full of body odour bouncing over bumpy terrain and having to look through a camera lens. If you were following in Captain Trunky and saw the FJ pull over and Juan quickly get out, you knew it was either to set up for a shot or to have a hurl. He was also the resident DJ, ensuring that the Beast and Captain Trunky were wired for sound at all times. A bit like an iceberg, you think you know him but then realize there is a whole lot more beneath the surface. It's great to see a man who's found his niche, is making the most of it, and loving it!

Dan Frost

THE MOUNTAIN GOAT

Dan, Dan, the Cameraman has been working in TV all his life, mainly as a freelance cameraman, and has been fortunate to travel the world, with the All Blacks and the Black Caps. But he reckons this was the job that has topped them all so far! Dan's highlight was climbing to 4000 feet up a muddy track with sheer drops on one side to then break through the mist and see the Stravon hunting lodge perched on the side of the mountain, overlooking a mass of native bush with a big waterfall as a backdrop. We nicknamed him the Mountain Goat or Steady-Cam because of his ability to run over the roughest ground, through creeks and streams, but the camera would remain perfectly still at all times. Like a stealthy assassin always shooting with deadly accuracy and precision.

Jared Burns

MR FIXIT

Jared was probably the most enthusiastic member of the crew, always up for anything. He formed a frighteningly close relationship with Captain Trunky and was pretty emotional when he had to kiss it goodbye when we got to Invercargill. He was blessed by not having to do much mechanical work on the trucks because they were indestructible. But he changed a few flat tyres, bent a door back into place, and most importantly disconnected the annoying beeping sound caused when the passenger seatbelt was not buckled up. But he came in handy for all sorts of odd jobs. It was like having a human Swiss Army knife with us. And he pretty gamely pushed the vehicles to the limit for nigh on nineteen days. He also provided in-house entertainment with his impersonations (possibly the pick of the bunch being Murray, the turnip farmer from Southland), his singing voice, and his love of Jimmy's Pies. Frankly, I reckon he was just stoked to get out of Palmerston North for a couple of weeks.

Morgan Dilks

SCOOP

While the rest of us had to fit in writing our emails and texts around the job, this was Morgan's actual job. But he did it bloody well, and earned the nickname Scoop because he'd upload photos and tweets minutes after the event. He was our primary link to the outside world. A calm, quietly spoken bloke, but you wouldn't want to piss him off. He's a karate master in his spare time. But being such a nice bloke it'd take a considerable amount to make him angry.

Luke Farmer

COOL HAND LUKE

Cool Hand Luke was the background workhorse and did all the important stuff like keeping the boot of Captain Trunky well stocked with beers, and he had the challenge of liaising with the TVNZ *Breakfast* crew. He was a toiler, though, doing all the extra hard jobs, like driving long distances to pick up supplies or dropping someone somewhere. Like Morgan, Luke was an excellent addition to the team.

James Brooks

GOLLUM
HOBBIT

Brooksie was one of the editors we affectionately nicknamed the Hobbits, due to their smallish stature, hairiness and nocturnal habits of staying up all night editing the footage. They had a diet of V and petrol station pies. The poor buggers basically had a ten- or twelve-hour commute to work in the back of a four-wheel-drive, occasionally helping to set up mini-cams. What Brooksie didn't know about the technical side of editing and computers basically wasn't worth knowing. He had this wicked server that he'd custom built for the trip and was pretty proud when talking us through it even though the only bloke who had any idea what it did or how it worked was Martin. He also brought along a satellite dish to upload clips remotely when we were stuck in out-of-the-way locations. A Yarpie by birth, we didn't hold that against him because he's such a positive and happy hobbit.

Martin Wilson

BILBO
BAGGINS
HOBBIT

A random but faithful hobbit, for the most part Martin kept his head down and worked hard. The hobbits spoke a language of their own, but they sure got the job done. Martin just loved being a part of one of the best roadies ever — the only part he didn't like was arriving in Invercargill and it all ending. Growing up on a Northland farm meant Martin was the perfect techie for the job as he could also deal with all the cockies we met en route. A good keen man who drinks his bourbon straight — not even on the rocks. Little wonder he's a hairy-chested hobbit. The hobbits loved the whole trip from inane jokes over the CB radio to playing hacky sack on the side of a country lane. Luckily, they required little food, as they often missed dinners with the crew because they were busy editing.

Charlie Haddrell
HADGE

Hadge was a bit of a lone ranger, joining the trip at Puhoi, then again in Wellington, and then riding shotgun from Queenstown via Dunners and the Catlins to Invercargill. Even then he'd often be running his own agenda, that is, until he got his white RAV4 rental nice and dirty when joining the team full-time for the last leg. When he gets into full swing he's one of the funniest jokers in the country and he was a great addition to the team, keeping us humoured during the tough final days of the challenge.

A REVOLUTIONARY MARKETING CONCEPT

The Top to Bottom concept was the brainchild of the above three gentlemen: Brett Hoskin, Creative Director, Aim Proximity; Neeraj Lala, GM Marketing, Toyota; and Mark Cochrane, Group Account Director, Saatchi & Saatchi.

In late 2010, I went out for dinner with Neeraj Lala, the General Manager of Marketing for Toyota New Zealand. He wanted to present the 'Top to Bottom' concept to me: the launch of the new FJ Cruiser, coinciding with the sixtieth anniversary of the first ever Land Cruiser. It was a truly fascinating conversation.

Toyota New Zealand has always prided itself on its marketing. The emotions, bonds and friendship with their customers are paramount. But when Neeraj came into the GM role, he quickly assessed the need for a far stronger collaboration between all of Toyota's marketing partners. He wanted his strong individual partners to gel and become a closer-knit part of the Toyota family. And he wanted them to cooperate on projects to achieve far greater results. He set about creating a culture and environment where agencies had the confidence to express their views fully and openly. He stressed that while some ideas may not fly, he encouraged ballsy thinking. He wanted to instil the 'Toyota Way' principles and practices in the processes of their marketing partners. Principles such as respect for others and the stimulation of teamwork, and practices such as continuous improvement.

So, early in 2010 Neeraj got all the marketing agencies together in Palmy North for what was called the Toyota Marketing Hui. The challenging (and yet interesting) thing with marketing these days is that it now has a lot of moving parts. So a month before the hui, Toyota briefed all the agencies with one joint task on the agenda for the hui. 'To celebrate sixty years of Land Cruiser in New Zealand we want an idea that allows Toyota to engage with our customers through the launch of the new FJ Cruiser.'

That month a lot of brainstorming sessions took place. Saatchi & Saatchi, Aim Proximity Wellington and Toyota were flat out working together, talking, dreaming, chatting. If you ask them no one really knows when it was invented, but apparently one morning the parties were discussing progress and it went something like, 'The truck is legendary, so what if we do something legendary, not just talk about it? ... What if we do a legendary mission in the FJ, film it and play it live online so people can control where to go? ... What if we drive the length of the country? Then someone said, 'What if we went from the top to bottom of New Zealand ... off-road? What if we meet customers along the way? What if we could rig a truck so people could watch it online?' That was the moment the idea was conceived.

Still, no one knew if it could actually be done, or what risks and assumptions needed to be made. But at the end of the Toyota Marketing Hui, the greater team stood up and presented an idea. 'FJ, Top to Bottom ... Off Road'.

The hour after that was when the magic happened. That was when everyone truly came together in a huge brainstorm. Scary questions were thrown around about whether it were possible, whether it would be allowed and how long it would take. But these three jokers stuck to their guns and said, 'Logistics aside for now, if you can dream it, you can do it.' And that's when 'FJ, Top to Bottom ... Off Road' was born.

I was highly impressed and eager to be part of such a revolutionary assignment. It turned out to be one of the most satisfying and amazing experiences of my life.

ACKNOWLEDGEMENTS

Idea and development by Team Toyota, Aim Proximity and Saatchi & Saatchi NZ.
Development by Team Toyota

Saatchi & Saatchi
Mark Cochrane
Luke Farmer
Steph Evans
Murray Streets
Brad Collet
Slade Gill
Ross Davies

Aim Proximity Wellington
Brett Hoskin
Sam Hember
Timothy Grieg
Craig Ballantyne
Mike Gwyther
David Buck
Donal Devlin
Ben Pujji
Julie Warmington
Simon Eathorne
Rudi Olckers
Mirko May
Ryan Christie

Wright Communications
Nikki Wright
Lester Thorley
Polly Atkins

Starcom
Susan Benseman

CONTENT PRODUCTION

Leftfield

SPONSORS

Toyota Financial Services
TVNZ
TRN
Telecom
DTM Wheels
The Mad Butcher